# The BOOK *of*
# REVELATION
# DECODED

### *REVISED EDITION*

## RABBI KIRT A. SCHNEIDER

CHARISMA
**HOUSE**

For more resources like this, visit MyCharismaShop.com and the author's website at DiscoveringTheJewishJesus.com.

Cataloging-in-Publication Data is on file with the Library of Congress.
International Standard Book Number: 978-1-63641-418-8
E-book ISBN: 978-1-63641-419-5

1 2024
Printed in the United States of America

Most Charisma Media products are available at special quantity discounts for bulk purchase for sales promotions, premiums, fund-raising, and educational needs. For details, call us at (407) 333-0600 or visit our website at www.charismamedia.com.

# CONTENTS

# SPECIAL THANKS

*I would like to thank my editor, Marcus Yoars, for his help in writing this book. His contribution was beyond that of a normal editor, and his impartation into this work was supernatural. Marcus, thank you!*

# PREFACE

IT HAS BEEN almost ten years since *The Book of Revelation Decoded* was first released. Since then, the signs of Jesus' return have only been increasing. My wife, Cynthia, and I were in Jerusalem on October 7, 2023, when Hamas attacked Israel. Like many around the world, I watched in horror as Iran bombed Israel with ballistic missiles and drones the following April. Whether those attacks are the beginnings of the end-time battle of Armageddon, one thing is certain: We are living in a preparatory period leading to the return of Yeshua (Jesus). It very well could happen in our lifetime, and we need to live as if it will.

That is why I am releasing a revised edition of this book. Today more than ever I believe the church needs to recognize what is happening and prepare for what is yet to come. The apostle Paul wrote:

> Now as to the times and the epochs, brethren, you have no need of anything to be written to you. For you yourselves know full well that the day of the Lord will come just like a thief in the night. While they are saying, "Peace and safety!" then destruction will come upon them suddenly like labor pains upon a woman with child, and they will not escape. But you, brethren, are not in darkness, that the day would overtake you like a thief; for you are all sons of light and sons of day. We are not of night nor of

darkness; so then let us not sleep as others do, but let us be alert and sober.

—1 THESSALONIANS 5:1–6, NASB

Paul is saying you and I are not in the darkness; we're not clueless. We're not walking around in deception, trying to save the whales while children are being murdered. No, we're the children of God, and we're aware of what is going on. We're not ignorant of the signs of the times. We see them flashing like neon lights pointing to Yeshua's imminent return.

Today we are experiencing what I call "the chaos of evil." People are defying God's created order, claiming gender is a choice and not biologically determined. Political division has reached such a fever pitch that many are anticipating another civil war in the United States. Liberals and conservatives are so far apart ideologically that reconciliation seems impossible, and the hatred is spilling into city streets.

Messiah Jesus said, "For nation will rise against nation, and kingdom against kingdom" (Matt. 24:7). The Greek word translated "nation" is *ethnos*, and it doesn't have to refer to a physical country. It can mean a people group or "side." So the verse is saying in essence that a people group or side will rise up against another people group or side, and the animus is becoming violent.

We're seeing confusion in the church, with fewer people connecting with local congregations as deception, discouragement, and distraction run rampant. Meanwhile, internet technology is being used to stifle any voices that aren't on board with the demonic agenda that has broken into the earth. And this is just the beginning. As much as things have changed in the last eight to ten years, they're going to change even more in the next eight to ten years.

The Bible tells us that "the mystery of lawlessness is already at work; only he who now restrains will do so until he is taken out of the way. Then that lawless one will be revealed whom the Lord will slay with the breath of His mouth and bring to an end by the appearance of His coming" (2 Thess. 2:7–8, NASB). Right now, the world is in a time of massive deception, and he that has been restrained is no longer being restrained.

Ten years ago, we wouldn't have imagined that artificial intelligence would be a reality and people would be using chatbots to stand in for friends and even romantic relationships. We wouldn't have thought a couple could lose custody of their son because he identifies as a girl and they refuse to refer to him using feminine pronouns. People are losing everything by taking a stand for issues that ten years ago were common sense. Beloved, Yeshua is getting ready to return.

If you read the previous version of *The Book of Revelation Decoded*, you will find much of the content unchanged. However, I have updated facts and statistics where necessary and included some additional insights in various places. My prayer is that after reading this book, you will prepare yourself for the difficult days to come so you can be ready to meet Yeshua at His return. Some of us are living in two worlds. On the one hand, we love the Lord, and on the other, we're entangled in sin. Now is the time to get right with God and fully surrender our lives to Him.

This is not a time for preachers to speak fluff and coddle the church. This is a time for the body of Messiah to be warned. I am releasing this revised edition as a way of indicating how important this message continues to be. While

this book is filled with important theological and escha-
tological information, it is primarily a wake-up call. I am
writing here to say, "Get ready!"

The good news is that where sin abounds, grace abounds
all the more, and God's grace is sufficient. We can live in intimacy with the Lord, and we can live in victory. But times are
only going to get tougher, and if we're not strong now, how
are we going to stand in the more challenging days ahead?

The time to get ready for the battle is not when you're in
the battle. It's before the fight. May this book prepare you for
the battle ahead so when you stand before the Lord in judgment, He will be proud of you for your love for Him and say,
"Well done, good and faithful servant! Enter the joy of the
Lord" (Matt. 25:21, 23).

INTRODUCTION

# THE REVELATION

ALL OVER THE world there is a sense of foreboding, a feeling that dark clouds are on the horizon. Like a murder of crows gathering overhead, the signs of trouble are not just looming; they continue to increase.

Terrorist attacks are becoming commonplace even in settings once thought off-limits for such atrocities. From the Hamas-led massacre on a music festival in Israel to mass shootings at concerts and synagogues and other festivals,[1] it seems no place is safe anymore. This is the new world war, fought not within continental boundaries but in shopping malls, concert arenas, movie theaters, and schools.

Meanwhile, faith in the world's major economies is struggling back after the sucker punch of the COVID pandemic and the global inflation that was left in its wake. Around the world, economic growth has remained sluggish, creating more skepticism and fear than hope.[2] Indeed, the World Bank estimates that the years since the pandemic have been "the slowest half-decade of GDP growth in 30 years."[3]

Of course there have always been times of economic uncertainty and threats of wars, so what makes today any different from other seasons in history? One answer to this is the imminence of nuclear destruction, as the single push of a button could wreak global havoc. The Iran nuclear deal of recent years continues to add fuel to the fire of a Middle East arms race.[4] Countries once weak and helpless against superpowers such as the United States and the former Union

1

of Soviet Socialist Republics (USSR) now have their hands on nuclear weapons or at least have access to nuclear power.[5] Some of the world's most unpredictable dictators of recent years—from North Korea's Kim Jong-un to the recently late Iranian president Ebrahim Raisi—made it a point to flex their country's nuclear muscles,[6] having in mind their two main enemies: the United States and Israel.

Cynthia and I had to take cover in a Jerusalem bomb shelter in the days following the Hamas terrorist attack on October 7, 2023, and we struggled to get a flight back to the United States. Of course, no one knows whether this will lead to Armageddon. But like many others, I believe it's possible events like these could be precursors to that climactic, end-time battle.

I have traveled often to Israel and have talked with many in the land. Years ago when I would ask about the country's morale—whether the average Israeli was hopeful or worried about the future—most Israelis possessed a remarkable sense of optimism. They had a strong belief that the Jewish people have always persevered no matter what obstacles or outside threats emerged. But this has been changing.

One tour guide I spoke with said he frequently had nightmares about his country. "Why would I not when every nation surrounding us has their weapons' sights set on us?" he asked. "We are staring down the barrel of their guns, and it's just a matter of time before they will pull the trigger." Not surprisingly, one study found the prevalence of PTSD, depression, and anxiety among Israelis nearly doubled in the weeks following the Hamas attacks.[7]

Such fear is not exclusive to Israel but now permeates the air around the world. In the United States seven out of ten adults say worries about keeping themselves or their families safe keeps them up at night.[8] A third of Americans fear a total economic collapse,[9] and 76 percent of Americans expect a massive global conflict involving the world's superpowers within the next twenty-five years.[10] According to one poll, more than 70 percent of people from roughly thirty nations think there is a very real threat of a nuclear, biological, or chemical attack happening in the next year, yet less than half (44 percent) think their governments are equipped to respond.[11]

For many people across the globe, the world is becoming an increasingly dangerous place, and they fear more trouble lies ahead.

## RECEIVING THE REVELATION

The Bible speaks at length of such mounting trouble in the Book of Revelation. The apostle John received a vision from God of the global calamity that would come in the last days, or what many refer to as the end times. He wrote down this vision under the guidance of the Holy Spirit, describing what he saw—from a climactic world war to cosmic signs of Earth's demise to strange creatures in heaven.

I doubt he knew his prophetic account would one day become one of the most controversial and misunderstood books of the Bible. Indeed, countless believers today avoid reading it because they think it is too difficult to understand, too scary, or, worse still, completely irrelevant.

It is true that the Book of Revelation contains some difficult elements. But for too long it has been seen as a confusing, mysterious, unapproachable book only to be understood by biblical experts. In fact, I have heard many Bible teachers preface their teachings on Revelation by saying only "mature believers" can truly understand its words.

I do not believe that God intended for this book to be understood by only a few. I am confident He wants every believer to receive the revelation of Revelation, no matter what his or her level of spiritual maturity or scriptural expertise. Its message is far too important—and yes, relevant—for the times we live in to be ignored, and that is especially true for believers.

That is why I have written this book—to present the content of Revelation with such simplicity and clarity that anyone can understand it and, as a result, the times in which we live. Jesus said of the Book of Revelation, "Blessed is he who reads and those who hear the words of this prophecy and keep those things which are written in it, for the time is near" (Rev. 1:3). This should let us know it is important to God that we understand the message given in this book.

In these pages we will examine the timeline of the main events discussed in the Book of Revelation and how they will unfold. My prayer is that knowing this will cause your expectation of Jesus' return to grow stronger and make you more determined than ever to live a godly lifestyle in anticipation of Messiah's coming.

Obviously there are parts of John's book that continue to confound Bible scholars almost two thousand years after its writing. But I believe by simply examining Revelation with Scripture itself—by using the lens of the Hebrew prophets—we can understand God's ultimate purpose for this crucial final book of the Bible: that it become a guide for the church in the last days to inspire, equip, and empower every believer. So whether you have studied God's Word for five weeks or fifty years, I believe the book you are now holding can help you grow in your faith and stand boldly in Christ in the difficult days ahead.

## THE END IS NEAR

As the signs of trouble increase around the world, many people are realizing that those sign-holding, megaphone-toting sidewalk prophets were right after all—the end *is* near. Their message, which most of the world ignored or mocked, is becoming reality. We truly are living in the last days.

How do we know this? How can I be so sure that such an overused prophecy has finally become truth? Won't the world naturally restore things to order just as it always does? Indeed, many people believe history is like a pendulum—when things swing too far to one extreme, the pendulum will inevitably swing the other direction to balance out everything. History proves that situations automatically fix themselves, they say.

This book will reveal that what we are experiencing today is not a pendulum effect. Immorality will not correct itself. Sin won't suddenly change its course. The pride of humanity—which we can see in everything from today's rise of atheism and secular humanism to our narcissistic, selfie-obsessed Western culture—will not willingly submit itself to defeat. No, nothing will happen that can reverse this progression of evil compounding evil. The global sense of impending doom will not pass. Indeed, things will go from bad to worse.

If that sounds too pessimistic for you or is too hard to believe, understand that Jesus warned us of this. More than two thousand years ago Yeshua HaMashiach, which is

Hebrew for "Jesus the Messiah," spoke in detail about what life would be like in the last days before He returned to earth. He outlined many of the events and situations that would compose what we refer to as the end times. The apostle Paul gave us more information about the end times in a few of his letters. And of course John, one of Jesus' original disciples, penned the greatest body of literature on the end times in the Book of Revelation.

But these accounts were certainly not the first to address the end times. Hundreds, even thousands, of years before, the Hebrew prophets of old spoke in detail about the last days. Many believers think of Revelation as *the* only end-times book in the Bible, yet they forget there are at least 150 chapters throughout God's Word in which the end times is the major topic.[12] The Book of Revelation is only 22 chapters, which means at least 128 additional chapters in the Bible do not just mention but discuss at length this pivotal time in history.

Often people do not realize how prominent the theme of the end times is in the Tanakh, which is the Hebrew Bible. The Tanakh is what believers know as the Old Testament and comprises three parts: the Torah (also known as the Five Books of Moses), Nevi'im (meaning "Prophets"), and Ketuvim ("Writings"). From the Tanakh's very first book, B'resheet (Genesis), the end times are part of the biblical story. In fact, even Jacob mentioned the last days when he gathered his sons, who would become the twelve tribes of Israel, to bless them on his deathbed: "Gather yourselves together, so that I may tell you what will befall you in the last days" (Gen. 49:1). So from Genesis to Malachi we find God revealing His plan for the end times to the Hebrew prophets.

One of the magnificent elements of the believer's Bible, then, is how the Old and New Testaments match up. This synchronization is both stunning and awe-inspiring. In Matthew 13:52, Yeshua said that "every scribe"—meaning a Jewish person in His day who knew the Torah and the prophets and who taught God's people—"who is discipled for the kingdom of heaven is like a man who is master of the household who brings out of his treasure new and old things."

That is exactly what I hope to do in this book—to bring forth the treasures from old and new things, from the ancient Hebrew Bible and from the New Testament, or what's called the B'rit Hadashah. When we compare scriptures from these side by side, we find a remarkable synchronism of God's plan spelled out in His Word. We also see that God is one and His Word is one—that the Bible is not two separate books but one continuous, progressive revelation that becomes clearer and clearer as time goes on. And when we interpret the Book of Revelation through the lens of the Hebrew prophets, using old and new to find treasures, we discover a new level of revelation.

## A New Expectation

Let's return to the question of the times in which we live. How do we know the end is near? Why am I so certain of this?

One reason is that we live in an era that has recaptured the spirit of the apostles. The early church and its leaders lived with a perspective that it was not a matter of *if* Jesus returned, but *when*. The writers of the New Testament possessed a constant expectation that Yeshua would return in their lifetime. We can tell by their writings that Paul and Peter, for example, did not think Jesus would *possibly* return in their lifetime; they were convinced that He *would* return during their lives.

In 1 Corinthians 1:7–8 Paul wrote, "You are not lacking in any gift while waiting for the revelation of our Lord Jesus Christ. He will strengthen you to the end, so that you may be blameless on the day of our Lord Jesus Christ." And in 2 Peter 3:12 Peter encouraged the early church "while [they were] waiting for and desiring the coming of the day of God." The Greek word used for *waiting* there is *prosdokōntas*, which means "expecting."[13] There was a communal sense of expectation shared among the early believers, and this unified them in a powerful way to live in constant preparation for the Messiah's return.

Today there is a clear sense of expectancy within the global church regarding the Lord's return. Such awareness had not been at the forefront of the church for a long time. In fact, for almost seventeen hundred years the church in general did not think much about the Messiah's return. As a result, we find little mention of the topic in the writings of church leaders such as John Calvin, Martin Luther, and John Wesley. The reason behind this relative silence is simple: The church understood that for Jesus to return, Israel must be in its land, in accordance with the Hebrew prophecies.

When Rome first conquered the Judean region in 63 BC, most Jews were still centralized in the area. But when the Romans destroyed Jerusalem and burned down the temple in AD 70 , the remaining Jews who were not killed were forced into slavery and exile. At that point messianic expectation immediately decreased—and remained as such until the miracle of May 14, 1948. That was the day the Jewish people were once again given their own land following the atrocities of the Holocaust, during which more than six million Jews were murdered.

Israel went from being an ancient idea to an actual nation born in one day, fulfilling Isaiah's prophecy from more than twenty-seven hundred years earlier in which he asked, "Who has ever heard of such things? Who has ever seen things like this? Can a country be born in a day or a nation be brought forth in a moment?" (Isa. 66:8, NIV).

This was an unforgettable day for the Jewish people. Those scattered around the world immediately began returning to the homeland—what's known as making aliyah in Hebrew— and fulfilling yet another prophecy, this time from Ezekiel 36:24: "For I will take you from among the nations and gather you out of all countries and will bring you into your own land."

This prophetic fulfillment continues today. Of the 15.7 million Jews around the world, 7.2 million live in Israel. In 2023 there were around 6.3 million Jews living in the United States, meaning there are more Jews now in Israel than in America.[14] Thousands more across the globe continue to make aliyah each year.

## SIGNS OF THE TIMES

Israel becoming a nation with its own land in 1948 was truly miraculous. The same can be said for when the nation recaptured Jerusalem in June 1967 following another stunning victory in the Six-Day War, despite being heavily outnumbered and vastly inferior in terms of arms, resources, and technology. For the average Israeli, these events stir a sense of patriotism and inexpressible joy that stand in stark contrast to the hopelessness of almost two thousand years of exile.

Yet these events and the phenomenon of Jews returning to the homeland mean something more for believers around the world—Jewish or not. For those who believe in Yeshua HaMashiach, these developments are blatant signs that we are indeed approaching the end times and that our Lord is soon to return. As a result, interest in eschatology, which is the study of the end times, is at an all-time high since the apostles' day. Jesus, Paul, John, and the Hebrew prophets all spelled out signs of the last days, yet these were all predicated upon Israel inhabiting the land. With that now being reality, I believe God is stirring His people worldwide to search the Scriptures and find His blueprints for the end times. He does not want us unprepared and overwhelmed when the events prophesied so long ago finally begin to unfold.

We will look at many of those events in this book. Specifically, we will examine more than twenty different elements associated with the end times. These are crises, events, developments, people, places, or things that hold tremendous significance in the context of the last days. Among them are:

- The great tribulation (what Scripture also calls "Jacob's trouble")
- The rise of the Antichrist
- The mark of the beast
- The abomination of desolation
- God's judgments and wrath (the seven seals, seven trumpets, and seven bowls)

- The rapture
- Armageddon
- The return of Jesus the Messiah
- The marriage supper of the Lamb
- Israel's salvation
- The ten lost tribes of Israel
- God's rewards
- The judgment seats
- The first and second resurrections
- Hell
- The lake of fire
- The Book of Life
- The millennial reign of the Messiah
- Satan's final assault
- The first heaven
- The new heaven and the new earth

Some of what I share on these topics will challenge your theology. Not only am I certain of this; I fully embrace it. I pray that you will wrestle with each topic and, more importantly, delve into Scripture in the same way I have. You may have been taught something different from what I will share in this book. For example, I do not think God will remove His church from the earth before the tribulation begins because I strongly believe that the Passover in Exodus is the prototype through which we must interpret the end-time events in Revelation. (I will explain this later.)

My goal in writing this book is not to persuade you on theological issues. Instead I want to show as clearly as

possible how the Old and New Testaments connect in relation to what they teach about the end times. I will do my
best to let those scriptures speak for themselves and allow
the power of God's Word alone to increase your faith.

Admittedly, though, some parts of Revelation can be difficult to understand. Because of this you may be tempted at
times to put down this book because you don't understand
what is being discussed. I will try to explain Revelation
as simply as possible, but I want to strongly encourage
you: *Don't give up!* Commit to reading through this entire
book—including the sentences, paragraphs, or parts you do
not understand on first pass. If you stick with it and perse-
vere in reading through the difficult parts, I promise that
although you may not understand every detail mentioned
in the Book of Revelation, by the end of this book you *will*
have a better grasp of John's account. More importantly, you
will have gained greater revelation into God's perspective for
how we as believers can face the times ahead with hope and
expectation.

We must be prepared with such hope and expectation
because, as you will discover in this book, we are entering
into the most difficult days in human history. What we today
think of as humanity's darkest moments—the Holocaust,
World Wars I and II, the Black Death, the Crusades, the
genocides of recent years—will pale in comparison with
what is yet to come. Amid such extreme darkness and evil,
a great deception will arise within the church, causing many
believers to fall away from their faith. The world will witness the most miraculous, supernatural signs and wonders
in history. And all throughout, the bride of Christ will be

purified and made spotless so she finally can be joined with her Bridegroom, Jesus, upon His return.

We will not automatically arrive at this place, however. It takes preparation. It takes us committing to being ready for the Lord's return at whatever hour. God wants to wake up His church so we can rise to face the difficult times that are ahead. Yeshua desires a bride who is ready and waiting, not one who is caught asleep during history's most pivotal moments.

As you read this book, I pray the Holy Spirit not only gives revelation and insight into His Word but also empowers you to stand strong for the coming days. May you be counted among those who, upon the Lord's return, hear Him say, "Well done, you good and faithful servant" (Matt. 25:21).

CHAPTER I

# JACOB'S TROUBLE: FROM TURMOIL TO THE GREAT TRIBULATION

WHAT'S SO SPECIAL about Israel? Why so much fuss for thousands of years over such a tiny speck of land? And why has the existence of such a relatively small group of people in the earth caused so much conflict?

As a natural-born Jew I have asked myself these questions many times. Both my parents are Jewish, and I grew up in the Jewish suburbs of Cleveland, Ohio, called Beachwood and Pepper Pike. Although Cleveland's Jewish population does not compare to that of New York City, Los Angeles, or Miami, it is still relatively large. In fact, Beachwood was almost 95 percent Jewish when my family lived there. So during my early years most of my friends, classmates, and neighbors were—you guessed it—Jewish.

That did not stop me from eventually realizing that I was different from others. As I grew older, I began experiencing more of the world beyond Beachwood. I noticed that at times Jewish people were seen or spoken to differently because of cultural stereotypes, and these views fueled an animosity toward Jews that has stoked the fires of anti-Semitism for thousands of years. Much of this hatred stems from the belief that because Scripture calls us God's "chosen people," we think of ourselves as special—and therefore better than others.

It is true that inherent in the Jewish identity is the sense that one is unique. But there is a major difference between uniqueness and superiority, and this is where most Jewish people have been misunderstood for so long. As one who is fully Jewish yet, by nature of my belief in Yeshua as the Messiah, ostracized by my own people, I know that I *am* different. I *am* unique. I also know that none of this really has anything to do with *me*. The same rings true for every Jewish person.

Whether you are a Jew or Gentile, it is critical to remember that God chose Israel. Israel did not choose God. In fact, history proves that time after time Israel rejected God and turned away from Him. And yet in His faithfulness He has not abandoned this chosen people. His covenant with the Jewish people is forever, and His love for them will never wane.

In the Book of D'varim (Deuteronomy) we find God pronouncing such faithful affection for His people while declaring their identity:

> For you are a holy people to the Lord your God. The Lord your God has chosen you to be His special people, treasured above all peoples who are on the face of the earth.
> —DEUTERONOMY 7:6

The prophet Amos reiterated that out "of all the families of the earth," the Lord singled out Israel (Amos 3:2). God calls the Jewish people the "apple of His eye" (Zech. 2:8). Is this because they did something special? Were they somehow holier and more worthy of His friendship than the rest of the world? No! It is simply because He *chose* them.

The question, then, is, why did He choose them? We find the answer early in the first book of the Tanakh (Old Testament), when God announced His plans to birth Israel during a conversation with His beloved servant Abraham:

> Now the Lord said to Abram, "Go from your country, your family, and your father's house to the land that I will show you. I will make of you a great nation; I will bless you and make your name great, *so that you will be a blessing.* I will bless them who bless you and curse him who curses you, and in you all families of the earth will be blessed."
> —GENESIS 12:1–3, EMPHASIS ADDED

Christians and Jews alike are familiar with this passage of Scripture and know it as the Abrahamic covenant. But too often we fail to realize that in it God was revealing His plan for all humanity, not just for Israel. From the very beginning God's plan was to bless the entire earth *through* Israel. This is absolutely crucial to understand, particularly as we begin to look at the Book of Revelation and the end times.

## THE CHANNEL OF GOD'S BLESSING

God's desire has always been for all people to enjoy what He originally created them for—perfect communion with Him—so they might live in the abundance of His blessings. Ever since humanity fell and brought sin into the earth, God has wanted to redeem His creation, and His means of doing this has *always* been through Israel. This is why He chose them. Again, there was nothing they did to warrant this selection; *He* picked them.

From the very birth of the Jewish people God revealed

His plan: that through them He would bless the world. Long before Israel came to be, the Lord spoke a profound covenant promise to Abraham:

> I will indeed bless you and I will indeed multiply your descendants as the stars of the heavens and as the sand that is on the seashore. Your descendants will possess the gate of their enemies. *Through your offspring all the nations of the earth will be blessed,* because you have obeyed My voice.
>
> —Genesis 22:17–18, emphasis added

God's plan of blessing and redemption culminated when He sent His only Son, Jesus, to save Israel. More than once Yeshua spoke of how He came first for the Jewish people. In Matthew 15:24 He told the Canaanite woman, "I was sent only to the lost sheep of the house of Israel." Earlier, when sending out His twelve disciples throughout Judea, He specifically instructed them, "Do not go into the way of the Gentiles, and do not enter any city of the Samaritans. But go rather to the lost sheep of the house of Israel" (Matt. 10:5–6). And elsewhere Yeshua clearly told the Samaritan woman at the well that "salvation is of the Jews" (John 4:22).

Why was Jesus so exclusive in pronouncing that He came for the Jewish people first? Because God had established a covenant that said He would bless all the nations of the world through the Jewish people! The Lord wanted to bless both Jew and Gentile. And the only way He could accomplish this for both, according to His own covenant, was to go through the Jewish people. He would not break that covenant.

Jesus was the very fulfillment of the Abrahamic covenant. Despite Israel rejecting Him as the ultimate blessing from

God, the Messiah's death and resurrection opened the way for "all the families of the earth [to] be blessed" (Acts 3:25). This is wonderful news for everyone; it is the good news of the gospel! But what I hope you can notice is that God did not stray from His plan to bless the earth through Israel, as was spoken to Abraham, and neither will He stray from this in the last days: His blessing comes *through* the channel of Israel.

That means Israel is intrinsically connected to the end times. In fact, Paul said Israel's salvation—the radical promise that "all Israel will be saved"—is a key component to the very clock by which the end times will play out (Rom. 11:25–26). God has appointed that for a time Israel will be partially hardened to the truth that Yeshua is its Messiah so that through their unbelief as many Gentiles as possible can have the opportunity to enter His kingdom (Rom. 11:11–12). Once again the world is blessed through Israel—even Israel's own unbelief in Yeshua HaMashiach!

We will discuss Israel's salvation more in a later chapter, but for now it is important to understand that Israel is not just a part of God's plan for the end times; Israel—as a people and a nation—is, in fact, at the center of Christ's return and the surrounding events. Israel has not lost its status as "the apple of [God's] eye." The Lord has not suddenly broken His covenant and changed His mind about His feelings for the Jewish people. On the contrary, He has woven them into the very fabric of His end-times plan for the earth to be redeemed. In fact, we find His promises for end-times Israel throughout the Tanakh and the B'rit Hadashah (New Testament), as we will discover more in this chapter and the coming chapters.

One of the most important of these promises, however, is not necessarily one of good news for Israel. Simply put, God promises trouble for Israel. *Great* trouble. Trouble so great that there has never been anything like it on earth before.

That doesn't sound too hopeful, now does it? And yet this is the starting point for our look into decoding the Book of Revelation.

## THE TIME OF JACOB'S TROUBLE

More than twenty-six hundred years ago the prophet Jeremiah issued the word of the Lord concerning Israel and the end times:

> For thus says the LORD: I have heard a sound of trembling, of fear, and not of peace. Ask now, and see, can a male labor with child? Why do I see every man with his hands on his loins, as a woman in labor, and all faces turned pale? Alas! for that day is great, so that no one is like it; *it is even the time of Jacob's trouble, but he shall be saved out of it.*
> —JEREMIAH 30:5–7, EMPHASIS ADDED

At first glance you may wonder what these verses have to do with the end times. How is Jesus' return to earth related to a "man with his hands on his loins" (v. 6), acting as if he were giving birth? Those familiar with Jeremiah 30 know the entire chapter deals with God's promise to restore Israel following the Jewish people's exile into Babylonian captivity. But the term "Jacob's trouble" is also a prophetic term that Jeremiah used to describe the tribulation that the nation of Israel will go through in the last days. Jacob's name was changed to Israel after he wrestled with God, and his twelve sons became the twelve tribes of Israel. These twelve tribes encountered great calamity when the Babylonians destroyed

Jerusalem in 586 BC, and then they were "saved out of" captivity, just as Jeremiah prophesied (v. 7).

But as is often the case with biblical prophecy, God's words have a twofold meaning and fulfillment in Jeremiah 30:5-7. In the same way Israel's days were "great" with trouble during its Babylonian captivity (v. 7), Israel will once again encounter great trouble in the last days. We know this because what Jeremiah referred to as "that day" is actually a shadow of Jesus' second coming. In fact, Paul used the same phrase more than six hundred years later to describe "when [Jesus] comes, *in that Day*, to be glorified in His saints and to be marveled at by all those who believe" (2 Thess. 1:10, emphasis added).

The day of the Lord's return is both a single day and a season surrounding that single day, and the Bible consistently paints it as a difficult time to be alive. If we think fear is running rampant today, we haven't seen anything yet! In fact, Jeremiah 30:5-7 essentially says that the "time of Jacob's trouble" will be so terrible that men will, as the prophet describes in verse 6, act like women in labor, grab their stomachs, and soil their pants! Grown men unable to control their bodily functions because they are so petrified? Now *that's* a terrible day!

The prophet Daniel, one of Jeremiah's contemporaries, reiterated how tumultuous this season will be in Daniel 12:1:

> And there shall be a time of trouble such as never
> was since there was a nation even to that time. And
> at that time your people shall be delivered, everyone
> who shall be found written in the book.

Like Jeremiah, Daniel spoke of a day of coming trouble unmatched by any other time in history. Regardless of what atrocities human history has included to this point, only one season can lay claim to such a description: the end times.

I can hardly imagine what it felt like for Jewish fathers and mothers during the Holocaust who had to walk naked with their starving young children into the firing lines or gas chambers of Auschwitz. I can barely comprehend what it was like to be a child abducted into the Lord's Resistance Army of Ugandan warlord Joseph Kony and forced to murder your own family members with a stick. But as horrific as these atrocities sound, what takes place during the end times will surpass every other time in human history.

Jesus Himself validated Daniel's account of the end times when, in Matthew 24, He gave the most detailed description of the last days in the New Testament outside of the Book of Revelation. In that chapter He even quoted from Daniel's writings, adding credibility to their authenticity. Speaking of Jacob's trouble, Yeshua said:

> For then will be great tribulation, such as has not happened since the beginning of the world until now, no, nor ever shall be. Unless those days were shortened, no one would be saved. But for the sake of the elect those days will be shortened.
> —MATTHEW 24:21–22

Sound similar? Indeed the words of Jesus, Daniel, and Jeremiah fit together like a hand in a glove. Jeremiah called this the "time of Jacob's trouble," and Daniel simply called it "a time of trouble," while Yeshua described it as one of "great tribulation." Despite more than six hundred years separating Yeshua from these Old Testament prophets, their prophetic descriptions of the calamity that will surround Israel in those days are almost identical. And when compared with the overall picture painted throughout the Book of Revelation, we find a perfect harmony between the Hebrew prophets of the Tanakh (Old Testament) and the writers of the B'rit Hadashah (New Testament).

## As in the Days of Noah

Yeshua added another element in His description of the end times in Matthew 24, one worth examining because of its increasing relevance today. In verses 37–39 He compared the last days to the time of Noah:

> As were the days of Noah, so will be the coming of the Son of Man. For as in the days before the flood, they were eating and drinking, marrying and giving in marriage, until the day Noah entered the ark, and did not know until the flood came and took them all away, so will be the coming of the Son of Man.

Though Jesus alluded to the end times on several occasions, Matthew 24 records His most detailed narrative of what this season will be like. It is worth asking, then, why out of any time in history He chose to compare the global climate during the end times to how it was when Noah lived. And that begs the question: What was it actually like during the days of Noah?

To find out, we need to go back to the Hebrew Bible, the Tanakh. There in the Book of B'resheet (Genesis), chapter 6, we discover the answer with a few succinct verses. We see that humanity's sinfulness was unbridled and ever-present:

The LORD saw that the wickedness of man was great on the earth, and that every intent of the thoughts of his heart was continually only evil. The LORD was sorry that He had made man on the earth, and it grieved Him in His heart....The earth was corrupt before God and filled with violence. God looked on the earth and saw it was corrupt, for all flesh had corrupted their way on the earth. So God said to Noah, "The end of all flesh is come before Me, for the earth is filled with violence because of them. Now I will destroy them with the earth."

—GENESIS 6:5–6, 11–13

Because the wickedness of humanity was so rampant and infectious, God had no other option but to destroy mankind and start over with Noah, who is described as "a just man and blameless among his contemporaries" (v. 9). For the sake of saving creation, the Lord *had* to begin again. And because His very nature is one of redemption, He had no other choice but to redeem the earth and humanity by starting from scratch with a prototype couple from every living creature.

One of the main purposes of the end times is to cleanse the earth of sin and unrighteousness. The judgments God will send are to purge the planet of its filth. Jesus will return to rid the earth of those who have made it "corrupt"—as in the days of Noah—with their unceasing wickedness. He will restore order to creation, establish His kingdom on earth as it is in heaven, and rule with His saints in a manner of peace and blessing—the likes of which the earth has not seen since before the fall.

I do not know exactly how close we are to the level of

wickedness on earth that will prompt Yeshua to return, but you don't need to be an expert in observing culture to see that morality today is much the same as it was in Noah's time. We celebrate violence and sexual immorality to the point that they have become mainstream entertainment. Just as the earth was "filled with violence" in Noah's day (Gen. 6:11), our world is literally filled with violence and sexual immorality being glorified on television, in movie theaters, on laptops, on tablets, on mobile phones, and on every other screen.

In centuries past people flocked to arenas to watch gladiators kill helpless victims because mankind's heart was evil; today we go to the movies and grab a bag of popcorn with a soda while watching people murder one another and commit every profanity imaginable. A three-year-old now has the ability to hold a handheld device in the middle of a church service and, with one wrong click or swipe, witness an orgy, decapitation, séance, rape, child sacrifice, or any other evil under the sun. Can you think of another time in history when such wickedness was so prevalent across the globe? In what other era did humans publicize and market their sin to the degree we do today?

## And "As It Was in the Days of Lot"

Clearly we suffer from moral blindness in that we cannot tell right from wrong anymore. Jesus didn't just mention the days of Noah when discussing the end times; He also alluded to the time of Lot and the cities of Sodom and Gomorrah.

> Likewise as it was in the days of Lot: They ate, they drank, they bought, they sold, they planted, they built. But on the day that Lot departed from

Sodom, fire and brimstone rained from heaven and destroyed them all. So will it be on the day when the Son of Man is revealed.

—LUKE 17:28–30

In Lot's time immorality in Sodom and Gomorrah had escalated so much that homosexuality was not just rampant; it was actually celebrated by all. Those who opposed it were chided for being judgmental, bigoted, and narrow-minded. (See Genesis 19:9.) Isn't it interesting how similar things are today?

My heart goes out to today's homosexual community. Many within it have been victims of what I believe are some of the world's greatest injustices. They have experienced levels of abuse, rejection, and hatred I cannot imagine, and I grieve for the pain many within the lesbian, gay, bisexual, and transgender (LGBTQ+) community carry. But the truth is that Jesus came to save them just as much as He came to save someone who struggles with overeating or pornography or lying.

And despite what pop culture says, there is a big difference between loving the homosexual community as Jesus would and saying that God accepts that kind of lifestyle. God does not approve of homosexuality; He calls it a sin, just as He calls lust, lying, hating, selfishness, gluttony, or murder a sin. (See Genesis 19:1–13; Leviticus 18:22; 20:13; Romans 1:26–27; 1 Corinthians 6:9.) But there is a reason the Bible records how the sin of homosexuality specifically warrants God's judgment—such judgment that He destroyed Sodom and Gomorrah with fire and brimstone because of it.

We know from the creation account that God made mankind "in His own image; in the image of God He created him;

male and female He created them" (Gen. 1:27). God fashioned us in His perfect image as either men or women, created for relationship with Him. Our masculinity and femininity are pure reflections of His likeness, and therefore they are inherent to our core identity. Stated another way, a person's most basic identity is in his maleness or her femaleness. When we defile our basic identity, then we defile God's very nature in us—and this is why homosexuality is such a deep issue. It distorts our God-given sexuality and says we can find our core identity in whatever gender *we* choose to be and through whatever gender *we* choose to express ourselves.

Let me reiterate that I love homosexuals, just as God loves them. God loves all people—period. I understand that many who are trapped in this lifestyle did not intentionally choose it. Some have been sexually abused; others lacked proper parental figures. And sin has affected all of God's creation. We are all sinners, whether we are homosexuals or liars or adulterers or prideful egotists. We all need forgiveness from our sins, and God offers that to us through Jesus Christ. But His redemptive plan does not change the fact that homosexuality is a sin, and the reason it invites God's judgment is because it defiles His original intent on the deepest level.

The world would have you believe that homosexuality is a hot-button issue in today's culture wars because the LGBTQ+ community needs more rights and should be treated with equality. But what is happening today is a far greater war in the spiritual realm that deals with the deeper issue of whether mankind's core identity is found in God or in ourselves. Satan has unleashed an all-out blitz to convince the nations that homosexuality is not a sin and that those who align with God's Word are narrow-minded bigots for trying to impose their archaic beliefs on today's more "modern" and accepting societies.

If you've noticed that the battle has only gotten more intense, consider this: Before Yeshua's first coming, the world was steeped in paganism and sexual immorality. But after Messiah Jesus came, Christianity began to spread from Judea throughout the Greek and Roman world. When the Roman emperor Constantine was converted to Christianity in the fourth century, he not only decriminalized Christianity but he also began to penalize immoral behavior, including homosexuality, which was eventually outlawed.

Before that time it was considered acceptable for men to have relations with whomever they wanted; by some accounts the vast majority of Rome's emperors engaged in homosexuality at least occasionally. But when Rome embraced the truth of Yeshua, a mass exorcism took place, and Western civilization was changed. We became grounded in Judeo-Christian values. The earth was exorcised of the demons that existed in barbaric nations before Jesus came. But Scripture reveals something interesting in Matthew 12:43–45:

> When an unclean spirit goes out of a man, it passes through dry places seeking rest, but finds none. Then it says, "I will return to my house from which I came." And when it comes, it finds it empty, swept, and put in order. Then it goes and brings with itself seven other spirits more evil than itself, and they enter and dwell there. And the last state of that man is worse than the first. So shall it be also with this evil generation.

Jesus tells His disciples that when a demon is cast out of someone, it looks for another body to inhabit, and when it doesn't find one, the spirit returns to its previous habitation. If the person hasn't cleaned up his life and gotten right with God, the demon will see an open door, a legal entrance, and step back in, but he will bring seven other demons that are worse than he.

Most people think of demons being cast out of individuals, but Jesus said "so shall it be also with this evil generation." I believe a generation, in Yeshua's mind, was the entire human race. This generation—humanity—will not pass away until the demons that were exorcised when Yeshua came return because of unrepentance, and those new demons are going to be worse than the ones originally cast out.

This is what I believe is behind the mass deception and confusion we are seeing today. Our culture does not just allow the sin of homosexuality; it approves of it and even presents it to our children as a holistic alternative. As in the days of Lot, society has become so morally corrupt that we have lost our moral compass, and we now call what is wrong right and what is right wrong. The prophet Isaiah warned about "those who call evil good, and good evil; who exchange darkness for light, and light for darkness" (Isa. 5:20). Yeshua offered the same warning to the generation in which sin runs as rampant as it did in Noah's and Lot's times. Why such a harsh warning? Because just as it was in those cases, the evil of that end-times generation will reach such a point that God *must* bring judgment.

## THE REALITY OF JUDGMENT

I believe we are living in that generation. I believe sin has reached such a level that people cannot tell the difference between right and wrong, and this eventually will usher in the wrath of God and the "great tribulation" Yeshua spoke of in Matthew 24:21. Now, a generation can last many years; I am not so naive as to think the wickedness of this world cannot get any worse than it is now.

Make no mistake, sin *will* continue to increase until the day of Yeshua's return. The infinite expressions of immorality will go from bad to worse.

But God will not let this go on forever. At some point He will step in and judge the world. This is not a myth. God's judgment is not just an idea, nor is the story of Noah just a fairy tale. In fact, one of the great phenomena anthropologists face regularly is that virtually every culture in the world has a catastrophic flood narrative woven into its history.[1] The details of these accounts may change, but each has the same underlying premise that long ago there was a great flood that came upon the world and destroyed humanity. How is it possible that all these different societies, cultures, and traditions—isolated from one another by huge bodies of water and having almost nothing in common—share the same account of a flood sent to destroy the earth? There is only one explanation: It really happened! Today archaeologists and scientists are discovering more and more proof that validates the flood.[2] Beloved, this is not made up; God most certainly judged the sinful world of Noah's time. And He will do it again.

The Bible is full of scriptures—from the Old *and* New Testaments—affirming the idea of God's future judgment upon those who will not receive Him. Throughout the Book of Isaiah, for example, we find references to the wrath poured out upon the whole earth on the Day of the Lord:

> See, the day of the LORD comes, cruel, both with wrath and fierce anger, to lay the land desolate, and He shall destroy its sinners out of it....I will punish the world for its evil, and the wicked for their iniquity; and I will cause the arrogance of the proud to cease, and will lay low the haughtiness of the ruthless. I will make a man more rare than fine gold...Therefore, I will shake the heavens, and the earth shall be shaken out of her place at the wrath of the LORD of Hosts and in the day of His fierce anger.
>
> —ISAIAH 13:9, 11–13

> The land shall be utterly emptied, and utterly despoiled, for the LORD has spoken this word.... The earth also is defiled by its inhabitants because they have transgressed the laws, violated the ordinances, broken the everlasting covenant. Therefore, the curse devours the earth, and those who dwell in it are held guilty. Therefore, the inhabitants of the earth are burned, and few men are left.
>
> —ISAIAH 24:3, 5–6

Revelation likewise speaks of angels releasing fire upon mankind during the great tribulation (Rev. 8:7–8; 9:15–18). God promises to exterminate sinners from the earth. Why would a loving God do such a thing? We will deal with this question extensively in a later chapter, but the more pressing issue is our current state of increasing wickedness.

People today are becoming more defiant against God, yet in His mercy He continues to withhold His full judgments. According to both history and biblical patterns, however, at some point something has to give.

This is what happened in Noah's time and what will happen in the end times. People will sin and reject God so much that their wickedness will be past the point of return. This will be humanity's own doing. At that point God will have no choice left but to destroy them so that He can start over, just as He did in Noah's time.

## The Early Signs

We are beginning to see signs of this impending judgment today. Yeshua assured us there would be signs to indicate that this time of judgment was arriving, and He specifically warned us that when we see these signs, it would be "the beginning of sorrows" (Matt. 24:8). Many Bible translations use the phrase *birth pains* in place of *sorrows*, giving a more vivid picture of childbirth. For a pregnant woman, the first indicators that her baby is about to arrive are painful. They also remind her that even greater pain lies ahead. So it will be in the last days, according to Jesus:

> For many will come in My name, saying, "I am the Christ," and will deceive many. You will hear of wars and rumors of wars. See that you are not troubled. For all these things must happen, but the end is not yet. For nation will rise against nation, and kingdom against kingdom. There will be famines, epidemics, and earthquakes in various places. All these are the beginning of sorrows. Then they will hand you over

to be persecuted and will kill you. And you will be hated by all nations for My name's sake. Then many will fall away, and betray one another, and hate one another. And many false prophets will rise and will deceive many. Because iniquity will abound, the love of many will grow cold.

—MATTHEW 24:5–12

Luke's account of end-times occurrences offers a few additional signs, including "signs in the sun and the moon and the stars; and on the earth distress of nations, with perplexity, the sea and the waves roaring" (Luke 21:25). In fact, in the very next verse the Lord spoke of "men fainting from fear and expectation of what is coming on the inhabited earth" (v. 26), much as Jeremiah's end-times prophecy described men grabbing their loins as if they were going to the bathroom in their pants (Jer. 30:5–7).

Entire books have been written about these end-times signs. I will not go into detail about each one, nor will I connect them to recent world events, as many authors have done. Instead I want you to see the profound connection between what the Hebrew prophets said about these signs and what the Book of Revelation states. Once again we find an incredible homogeneity between the two. Let's look at a couple of these signs to see this parallel in action.

### Earthquakes

One of the telltale signs of the end times that Jesus mentioned is earthquakes. Seven hundred years prior, the prophet Isaiah predicted that in the last days the Lord will shake the entire earth.

For the windows from on high are open, and the foundations of the earth shake. The earth is utterly broken down, the earth is split through, the earth is shaken violently. The earth reels to and fro like a drunkard, and it totters like a shack, and its transgression is heavy upon it, and it shall fall, never to rise again.

—ISAIAH 24:18–20

John also spoke of a great earthquake in Revelation 16, which appears to be the same one Isaiah prophesied about:

And there were noises and thundering and lightning and a great earthquake, such a mighty and great earthquake, as had never occurred since men were on the earth. The great city was divided into three parts, and the cities of the nations fell.

—REVELATION 16:18–19

And Revelation 6:12 mentions yet another shaking of the earth:

I watched as He opened the sixth seal. And suddenly there was a great earthquake.

—REVELATION 6:12

## Cosmic phenomena

Along with warning us of massive earthquakes, Jesus also pointed out that "signs in the sun and the moon and the stars" will usher in the end times (Luke 21:25). Much has been made in recent years about blood moons, full eclipses, and other cosmic signs—and particularly their connection with the timing of certain Jewish holidays, stock market crashes, and man-made disasters. Although I will leave these types of predictions to others, I do know that the ancient prophets of the Old Testament and Yeshua foretold unusual and disturbing phenomena taking place in the heavens in relation to the times preceding Jesus' return. Speaking of the end times, the prophet Isaiah said:

> For the stars of heaven and their constellations shall not give their light; the sun shall be dark when it rises, and the moon shall not cause her light to shine.
>
> —Isaiah 13:10

Joel also specifically mentioned a cosmic darkness as a sign of the last days:

> All the inhabitants of the earth will tremble, because the day of the LORD has come, because it is near—a day of darkness and gloom, a day of clouds and thick darkness....The sun will be turned to darkness, and the moon to blood, before the great and awe-inspiring day of the LORD comes.
>
> —Joel 2:1–2, 31

Just as Jesus affirmed Daniel's end-times prophecies, He also confirmed Joel's when He paraphrased Joel 2:31 in Matthew 24:29:

> Immediately after the tribulation of those days, "the sun will be darkened, the moon will not give its light; the stars will fall from heaven, and the powers of the heavens will be shaken."

These and other mentions by the Hebrew prophets line up perfectly with what John saw in the Book of Revelation:

> I watched as He opened the sixth seal. And suddenly there was a great earthquake. The sun became black, like sackcloth made from goat hair, and the moon became like blood. And the stars of heaven fell to the earth, as a fig tree drops its unripe figs when it is shaken by a strong wind.
>
> —REVELATION 6:12–13

Can you see how all these scriptures continue to match up? Do you see how the Hebrew prophets' words perfectly synchronize with what is revealed in the New Testament? I hope this is increasing your faith and that you are starting to comprehend more of God's master plan for the world. Again, this is not some myth or fairy tale. This is the reality of what lies ahead.

Joel, Isaiah, Jeremiah, Ezekiel, and Jesus all spoke the exact same thing, which was then confirmed by the vision given to John on the island of Patmos in the Book of Revelation. This alignment is not some coincidence; this is by God's design. And when we understand that the Hebrew Bible is the foundation of our faith—that it all points to and is fulfilled in Yeshua HaMashiach—then the roots of our faith will undoubtedly grow deeper.

## GOOD NEWS AMID GROWING TROUBLE

What begins as a time of trouble for Israel will turn into global turmoil and, as Yeshua taught, escalate into the great tribulation—a season in which God's judgments are poured out and His full wrath eventually covers the globe. Whether we like that message matters little; it is the truth, as foretold by the Hebrew prophets thousands of years ago. Simply put, judgment *is* coming!

But I would not be telling the whole story if I stopped there—and thank God for that! Until the actual day of Jesus' return, God will extend His mercy and provide a way out from His judgment. We or our loved ones do not have to be among those whose hearts become so hardened that turning back is impossible. That is why Hebrews 3:15 reminds us, "Today, if you will hear His voice, do not harden your hearts as in the rebellion." It is by God's grace and mercy that His final judgments have not already come and that there is still time to repent and turn to Him.

This is the wonderful, glorious gospel—the good news— namely, that we have a way out through Jesus the Messiah. When we come to Him in repentance, confessing our sinful state and our need for Him as Lord and Savior, He saves us. When Jesus died on the cross at Calvary, He took the punishment we each deserve. First Peter 2:24 says, "He Himself bore our sins in His own body on the tree, that we, being dead to sins, should live unto righteousness." Second Corinthians 5:21 says, "God made Him who knew no sin to be sin for us, that we might become the righteousness of God in Him."

To use a layman's definition, righteousness is simply *right standing with God*. Because of Jesus' sacrifice we have been made right with God and returned to the place where He originally created us to be: in perfect fellowship with Him. Through Yeshua we have been saved, not just for today, but also for the coming times of trouble. As the writer of Hebrews says, "Christ was offered once to bear the sins of many, and He will appear a second time, not to bear sin but to save those who eagerly wait for Him" (Heb. 9:28).

This is glorious news for those who put their trust in Jesus. But it is also terrifying news for anyone who rejects Him. At some point time will run out. One day it will be too late. When Jesus returns, there will be no more chances to turn back. And even He said, "Concerning that day and hour no one knows [when it will be], not even the angels of heaven, but My Father only" (Matt. 24:36).

That alone should wake us up—both believers and non-believers—and keep us alert. If you have never confessed Jesus as Lord and Savior, let this truth be the alarm that brings you to God in repentance. The Lord will still respond with mercy in this hour.

And for those of us who already know Him, I pray it shakes us to the point where we are compelled to share the good news of what He has done for us with those who have not heard. I pray that out of this reality we approach every day and every hour with a renewed commitment to living "in a manner worthy of the Lord" (Col. 1:10). This is not the time to be entangled in sin. This is the time to break loose of immorality—to be free of addictions and affairs—and set our eyes upon the Lord.

Yeshua has warned us in the past, and He is once again warning us today that He is coming back. Jacob's trouble is on the horizon. Now is the time to get ready!

# CHAPTER 2

# WHEN THE ANTICHRIST WILL RISE

O N THE WESTERN outskirts of Jerusalem, atop the lush green slope of Mount Herzl, lies one of Israel's most valuable possessions. Yad Vashem, the main Holocaust remembrance center in the world, contains haunting memories from less than a hundred years ago, yet the lessons contained within it must last forever. Tourists to the site agree it is one of the most important parts, if not the most emotional part, of their visit to the Holy Land.

I have been to Yad Vashem several times, and I've watched people leave the site with the same multifaceted look staining their faces. Bewildered. Grieved. Angry. Exhausted. Puzzled. Astounded. They all have the same thought in mind—in fact, I have heard many express it aloud.

*How? How could this happen?*

That same question is what we all ask whenever we uncover more stories, more information, more disgusting details of the worst period in Israel's history. And, of course, the more we uncover about the Holocaust, the more questions are raised.

How could human beings commit such inhumane acts? How could the world sit by and do so little knowing that millions of Jews were being murdered? How could young soldiers stand and laugh while watching innocent children suffer so brutally? How could a supposed Christian nation— the same nation that gave us the Reformation—have such hatred toward the people their God said He loved so much? How could one man stir a nation into such a demonic frenzy? *How? How? How?!*

We are still answering these questions today. Even with the ongoing call for restitution that has led to a handful of ninety-plus-year-old former SS guards being convicted, many of our questions surrounding the Holocaust may never be answered this side of eternity.[1] Yet one thing we *can* know is how one of history's deadliest men rose to power in the first place and created such hell on earth. The relatively slow ascent of Adolf Hitler to his place as the world's most powerful man is a sobering reminder of how vulnerable we are today to yet another Satan-driven global leader ushering in another era of genocide.

## HITLER'S RISE TO POWER

As early as 1920 Hitler was addressing large audiences, promising economic recovery for a Germany crippled by defeat in World War I.[2] Hitler knew how to stir and manipulate the masses in his speeches like few other orators in history, and even during his early political years witnesses remarked at the almost spiritual euphoria he induced in crowds.[3] His promises of peace, prosperity, power, and a return to Germany's glory days left listeners spellbound and whipped into a nationalistic frenzy. Meanwhile, because his rise to prominence was slow—from leading a tiny Nazi party in 1921 to becoming the country's all-powerful führer and chancellor in 1934—his extreme anti-Semitism gradually became more acceptable even for those who held no disdain for the Jewish people.

From his earliest days in politics Hitler never hid his

hatred for the Jews and continued to incite crowds with the idea that the Jewish people were to blame for all Germany's problems—indeed all the world's problems. In *Mein Kampf*, Hitler's 1925 book presenting his political ideology and future plans for Germany, he referred to the Jews as filthy and compared them to maggots while accusing them of contaminating the pure blood of Germans, as well as every other race.[4]

Hardly anyone said a word to object. Instead, the crowds kept on cheering, too entranced by his promises to restore their personal well-being to worry about the welfare of millions who would soon be in danger. It was not until this madman had gained complete authority that he quickly revealed just how sinister he was in his uncompromising plan to exterminate the Jewish people.

## ANOTHER WORSE THAN HITLER?

This is not the last time we will see the rise of such a satanically driven leader. Nor is it the last time such a powerful leader will manipulate the masses in an attempt to eradicate the Jewish race. The Bible promises that in the end times the Antichrist will rise to power in much the same way Hitler did during the 1920s and 1930s, only more quickly. And this global leader's goal will go beyond just killing Jews; he will want every Jew and believer on the face of the earth dead.

The truth is, Adolf Hitler was typecast as the Antichrist, or the Anti-Messiah. Though he had several characteristics that we know the Antichrist also will possess, Hitler was a mere foreshadowing of a far greater one to come. Jesus warned us of "false christs and false prophets" (Matt. 24:24), but these are different from the person we will look at in detail in this chapter and the next one. First John 2:18 says, "As you have heard that the antichrist will come, even now there are many antichrists." Hitler was certainly one of these antichrists, but he was not *the* Antichrist.

Both the Tanakh (Old Testament) and the B'rit Hadashah (New Testament) have much to say about the Antichrist, including what he will do and the times in which he will appear. Though I will not attempt to predict who the Antichrist is, I do want to illuminate the moral and social conditions that will allow him to arise and, more specifically, what the Tanakh and the B'rit Hadashah say about what will take place on earth when he emerges.

I believe these things are important for believers to know because, as is the case with God's judgments, we must be ready for the hour in which they come. God has given us a guide for the end times: the Scriptures. We must be discerning then, armed with the knowledge of Scripture, to avoid succumbing to a power that will be far greater than that of Nazi Germany, because for all the wisdom and intelligence we think we have gained since Hitler's rise to power, the world will be duped again. Millions will succumb to the promises of the Antichrist. In fact, many in the church will think he is the Messiah who has come to bring peace to the earth—that's how convincing he will be. But we must be discerning like the sons of Issachar in 1 Chronicles 12:32, "who understood the times and knew what Israel should do" (NIV). We must have such understanding to stand strong in the Lord during the trying times ahead.

## WHEN SIN HAS RUN ITS COURSE

Two questions often emerge whenever people discuss the Anti-Messiah: *When* will he appear, and *how* will he rise to power? We will tackle the first of those questions in this chapter. Because we can now look back in history and trace the emergence of such antichrists as Hitler, believers assume we will be smart enough to recognize exactly when the Antichrist will show up on the global scene. And since society is still aghast at how someone as evil as Hitler could rise to power and murder so many, we assume we will be able to prevent such an ascent, even if it is the Antichrist.

The truth is, no one but God will be able to stop the rise of the Antichrist, and when the Lord puts an end to him, He will have used this tool of Satan to accomplish His master plan to cleanse the earth of lawlessness. For those who want to be prepared for this time, knowing what Scripture has to say about *when* the Antichrist appears is intricately connected to *how* he shows up. So let's tackle the timing question first.

In Daniel 8 the prophet makes a profound statement that reveals much about God's divine timeline for the earth. It often gets lost, however, amid his detailed description of the Antichrist and the end times.

> In the latter time of their kingdom, when the transgressors have reached their limit, a king will arise, having a fierce countenance, skilled in intrigue. His power shall be mighty, but not by his own power. And he shall destroy wonderfully and shall prosper and practice his will and shall destroy the mighty men and the holy people. By his cunning, he shall

cause deceit to succeed under his hand, and he shall
magnify himself in his heart. He shall destroy many
in a time of peace. He shall also rise up against the
Prince of princes; but he shall be broken, not by
human hands.

—DANIEL 8:23–25

Did you catch that? When will the Antichrist appear?
(Hint: It's in the very first verse.) "*When the transgressors
have reached their limit,* a king will arise." There are many
variations in how this phrase from verse 23 is translated. The
New International Version says, "when rebels have become
completely wicked." The New Living Translation states,
"when their sin is at its height." The New American Standard
Bible puts it this way: "when the transgressors have run their
course." And the Holman Christian Standard Bible trans-
lates it as, "when the rebels have reached the full measure of
their sin."

However you translate this phrase, the meaning is
obvious: Sin and wickedness will have run their course
and finally, after thousands of years, reached an end point.
That means there will be no more capacity to be sensitive to
sin. Mankind's conscience will have been seared—yes, that
is how evil the world will be. At that point, when sin has
reached its maximum, the Anti-Messiah will show up and
appear to save the day. He will come when people on earth
have become so saturated with darkness and when evil is
so abundant—when there's such a demonic stronghold and
Satan has such reign on the earth—mankind will no longer
be able to tell the difference between right and wrong. They
will be incapable of detecting such darkness in a global

leader because the entire world—including themselves—will be so darkened by sin.

In the previous chapter we looked at past examples of when the world had grown this dark. In Noah's time the world was so filled with violence that it corrupted the planet. In Lot's time Sodom and Gomorrah were so overrun by sexual immorality that the cities' men threatened to kill Lot if he prevented them from having sex with the angels visiting him. In our time more people are enslaved than ever in history, and each year as many unborn babies are murdered as American soldiers have been killed in all wars combined.[5] We celebrate our immorality by marketing it as entertainment, and we even bless such immorality in our churches when we approve of homosexuality.

How dark is dark enough? Daniel says this "king" will arise when sin has run its course. I wonder, are we almost to that point now? And will we have the ability to detect the Antichrist amid all the darkness?

## HARDENED HEARTS

The answer to this last question lies in the New Testament counterpart to Daniel's words. It is an important passage, filled with theological depth and found in the very last chapter of Revelation. An angel of the Lord informs John that the end times are "at hand" and then tells him this:

> He who is unjust, let him be unjust still. He who is filthy, let him be filthy still. He who is righteous, let him be righteous still. He who is holy, let him be holy still.
>
> —REVELATION 22:11

At first glance this is a puzzling verse. Is God really telling those who sin to keep on sinning? Doesn't He want them saved and cleansed—to be just, righteous, and holy so they can stand in His presence? Usually you would expect the Lord to say something like, "Turn to Me, repent, and you shall be saved." But that is not what He seems to be indicating here. So why would God say such a thing?

God sees all and knows all. He knows our hearts; He knows when we say one thing but actually believe something else. He knows when we do all the right things on the outside to look good yet have hearts full of sin on the inside. So He alone knows when people have reached a point of no return or when they've permanently hardened their hearts against His grace. This is why we find Scripture at times saying that God "hardened" someone's heart.

For example, when God sent the ten plagues on Egypt, Exodus 9:12 records that "the LORD hardened the heart of Pharaoh, so that he did not listen." Many atheists and non-believers point to such passages as proof that God is neither just nor loving. After all, what loving God would cause someone to defy Him, only to punish that person for such defiance?

What these critics conveniently forget is that, as we see in only a few verses prior, Pharaoh's heart was already hard on its own, without any assistance from God (Exod. 7:13, 22; 8:15, 19, 32; 9:7). It was already hard for years—maybe decades—before when he kept more than one and a half million Jews enslaved and subjected to horrendous oppression and abuse.[6] If this was the same Pharaoh living when Moses was born, then his heart had already been hard enough to command that every Jewish male newborn should be murdered

(Exod. 1:16). So when God told Moses He would harden Pharaoh's heart, He was solidifying what was already there.

In his letter to the Roman believers, the apostle Paul expands on the reason the Lord did this:

> For the Scripture says to Pharaoh, "For this very purpose I have raised you up, that I may show My power in you, and that My name may be proclaimed in all the earth." Therefore He has mercy on whom He wills, and He hardens whom He wills.
>
> —ROMANS 9:17–18

God's perspective is infinitely higher and more complex than anything we can think of with our finite human minds. Therefore only He can deem what is truly necessary for His name to be "proclaimed in all the earth" (v. 17). This is the same mystery revealed in God's end-times plan. The Lord will use even the evil of man and Satan himself to do the greatest good. He will allow Satan to empower the Antichrist to deceive many in order to accomplish His higher will. Like Pharaoh, these deceived individuals are ones whose hearts are already hardened, who have rejected God's mercy and love, and who have taken "pleasure in unrighteousness," as 2 Thessalonians 2 explains when speaking of the Antichrist's emergence in the end times:

> For the mystery of lawlessness is already working. Only He who is now restraining him will do so until He is taken out of the way. Then the lawless one will be revealed...even him, whose coming is in accordance with the working of Satan with all power and signs and false wonders, and with all deception of

unrighteousness among those who perish, because
they did not receive the love for the truth that they
might be saved. Therefore God will send them a
strong delusion, that they should believe the lie: that
they all might be condemned who did not believe
the truth but had pleasure in unrighteousness.
—2 THESSALONIANS 2:7–12

The Bible proves that when people harden their hearts
against God to the point of no return, He will no longer
strive with them and instead will allow them to suffer the
consequences of their own sinfulness. (See Genesis 6:3.) To
those living in the end times who refuse His mercy, God
will "send them a strong delusion, that they should believe
the lie" (2 Thess. 2:11). What lie was Paul talking about? The
lie of the Antichrist spirit! In other words, in the end times
people will believe the lies and propaganda the Antichrist
spreads about himself, and these people will be among the
ones duped into believing he is the world's savior. Remember,
these are also the ones who have already rejected God's truth
and wallowed in their sin. God is simply giving them what
they asked for and allowing them to believe their own lies.

Can you see now why God says in Revelation 22:11, "He
who is unjust, let him be unjust still. He who is filthy, let
him be filthy still"? Again, God sees the bigger picture; He
knows the end from the beginning and has a perfect plan
for the last days. God has declared in His Word that Yeshua
HaMashiach will not return until the Antichrist appears.
The Lord *wants* to return, but He has conditioned His return
upon the Antichrist's arrival. And the Antichrist's arrival, as

we read in Daniel 8:23, is conditioned upon sin running its course—"when the transgressors have reached their limit."

I can imagine the Lord's heart was filled with longing when He had the angel tell John those words in Revelation 22:11. Yeshua deeply desires to return. He knows the sooner that day comes, the sooner His beloved bride, the church, can be reunited with Him and the sooner the earth can be cleansed and, eventually, a new heaven and new earth established.

Though it sounds strange, the Lord wants sin to reach the end of its course so the Anti-Messiah can come—so He can step in, destroy the Antichrist, eradicate sin from the earth, set up His kingdom in this world, and make things right once again. This is why we say, "Maranatha!," which is the Aramaic word meaning "Lord, come!"[7] And this is exactly why John writes in Revelation 22:17, "The Spirit and the bride say, 'Come.'" Come, Lord Jesus!

# CHAPTER 3

# HOW THE ANTICHRIST WILL RISE

IN THE PREVIOUS chapter we answered the question of *when* the Antichrist will appear. Now let's address the question of *how* he will rise to power—because the timing of the Antichrist's appearance will actually explain how he is able to ascend so easily.

As already mentioned, we wonder today how it was even possible for someone as evil, demented, and psychopathic as Hitler to gain such extreme power over so many people. Yet we know at least two reasons for his ascent in the years preceding World War II: First, Germany became morally bankrupt enough to allow such an immoral dictator to continually gain power, and second, the nation was completely desperate for change of any sort. I believe these are the exact same conditions among the masses that will allow the Antichrist to make such a rapid rise to power among the nations.

Hitler's rise in the 1920s came during Germany's darkest days following World War I. War reparations handcuffed the German economy and led the government into bankruptcy. With hyperinflation affecting families of all economic classes and leadership desperate for a solution, Germans were more willing to compromise their morals. This set the stage for Hitler's scapegoat ideology of blaming the Jewish people for all the country's woes.[1]

As his Nazi party gained power, the nation's ability to distinguish right from wrong deteriorated. A cycle of moral decline developed: The more desperate people became for a savior—anyone to make life better for them—the more they were willing to sacrifice their morals to be pulled out of the mire. So as desperation and moral bankruptcy fed each other, Hitler began a carefully plotted campaign to strip German Jews of everything.

First, the anti-Semitic fires that already existed in universities, the media, and other pockets of German society during the 1920s were fanned into flame with the nationwide boycott of Jewish businesses and professionals in 1933.[2] Few people publicly objected the next year when Hitler purged all political opposition. When Hitler was declared supreme leader and chancellor of Germany, national fear of the Nazi party and its ruthless SS force grew to the point that the average German dared not speak up against Hitler's policies and his increasing persecution of the Jewish people.[3]

By the time Jewish families were being carted off like cattle into freight trains and "relocated" to concentration camps, the nation's moral compass was officially broken. Add to this an entire generation of young people desperate for some sense of power, and Hitler now had a military force he could train to be immune to issues of morality.

What else can explain how, by 1940, soldiers were tossing Jewish babies in the air for target practice or silencing crying infants by smashing their heads against the side of a truck?[11] Only a morally blind society, filled with violence and wickedness, could allow such things, much less approve of them.

Beloved, as horrible as these examples sound, the Bible is clear that the world is heading for something even worse. Jesus said that we are approaching a time so difficult that there has never been another time like it, nor will there be another time like it again. It is called the tribulation (Matt. 24:21).

Today we are not far from being just as morally bankrupt as Germany became under Hitler. Even now our society is losing all sense of morality as we call what is right wrong and what is wrong right. (See Isaiah 5:20.) This is not just in the United States. Throughout Europe, South America, Asia, Africa, and Australia immoral agendas continue to make headway in turning sinful actions into part of mainstream culture.

In the previous chapter we addressed the issue of homosexuality, but there are many other issues being driven by demonic powers. How else could we justify the murder of more than sixty-three million unborn babies since 1973—and call it "women's reproductive rights"?[4] Or what else can explain how entire industries are now built around keeping people addicted to prescription and illegal drugs, pornography, gambling, and the like? This is all just exaltation of the individual above the Creator and His absolute moral code. Clearly, we are in moral freefall.

Meanwhile our desperation for a savior grows as the world becomes more chaotic. Economic uncertainty has made many nations desperate for any signs of stability or hope. The spread of terrorism and the proliferation of nuclear weapons continue to create global fear. Hamas' attack on Israel in 2023 and Iran's subsequent bombing of the nation have left many wondering if we're heading into World War III. Add to that Russia's invasion of Ukraine and Russian President Vladmir Putin's threat to use nuclear weapons against Western nations that get further involved in the conflict.[5] People are desperate to feel safe and secure. This is all creating an environment for someone to rise to power. It is paving the way for a charismatic figure who can inspire people and give them a sense of hope and security.

Enter the Antichrist.

The Antichrist will gain approval by appearing to be a man of peace and love amid a world filled with violence and hate. Nations will be desperate for anything to stop the riots, social unrest, and financial crises within their borders. The unending calamity will make them open to any leader who appears to have a real solution, someone who is seemingly heaven-sent and will save the day.

And that is *exactly* who the Anti-Messiah will seem to be.

## THE ANTICHRIST'S APPEAL

If you could blend Hitler's oratory skills with Alexander the Great's military mind, Franklin D. Roosevelt's popularity, Abraham Lincoln's humanitarianism, Martin Luther King Jr.'s courage, and Napoleon's cunning, you would only scratch the surface of what the Antichrist will appear to be as a leader. He will, by all scriptural accounts, be the smoothest-talking, most powerful, likable, and charismatic deceiver the world has ever seen. For a season his global appeal and popularity will be unmatched.

Amid a world at the apex of its sin, wickedness, chaos, violence, disorder, disease, and dysfunction, the Antichrist will appear and usher in a season of peace and unity throughout the planet. He will seem like the savior everyone has been waiting for, who has all the answers. Daniel 9:27 indicates that the Antichrist will even perform a miracle for the ages by bringing about peace in the Middle East through a seven-year "covenant" with Israel. (We know this pact eventually will be broken, however, and his true hatred for Israel revealed.)

The Antichrist will appear even more peaceful and loving than believers because he will embrace everything in the name of tolerance. He will welcome every religion, every life-style, every form of sexuality, and every definition of marriage and family. Society will praise him for such humanitarianism and compassion while labeling believers as narrow-minded, judgmental, hateful bigots. After all, we will be the ones who continue to point out the boundaries between right and wrong and thus be thought of as intolerant and divisive. Under the Antichrist's one-world government, taking a biblical stance will be labeled a hate crime and eventually become the impetus for persecuting countless believers.

We can already see traces of this today, where a Christian couple in Indiana lost custody of their child because they refused to use feminine pronouns to refer to their son, who identifies as a girl;[6] where Christian parents in Germany have been imprisoned and fined for withholding their children from sex-education classes that teach nine-year-olds how to have sex (including homosexual sex); or where medical staff in Sweden and Poland have been fired or denied jobs for refusing to perform abortions because of their faith.[7] Around the world pastors and clergy are feeling the heat for refusing to perform same-sex weddings, and it is simply a matter of time before most countries penalize dissenters with jail time.

Indeed by the time the Antichrist shows up, believers will have already experienced great persecution. Yet Satan will empower the Antichrist in an all-out assault from hell upon God's people.

Satan's goal has always been to destroy God's children, and in Revelation 12 John gives a detailed picture of the age-old conflict involving God, a dragon (Satan), a woman

(Israel), the child she bore (Jesus), and the remnant of her offspring (believers).

> The dragon [Satan] stood before the woman [Israel] who was ready to give birth, to devour her Child [Jesus] as soon as He was born. She gave birth to a male Child [Jesus], "who was to rule all nations with an iron scepter." And her Child [Jesus] was caught up to God and to His throne....When the dragon [Satan] saw that he was cast down to the earth, he [Satan] persecuted the woman [Israel] who gave birth to the male Child [Jesus]....Then the dragon [Satan] was angry with the woman [Israel], and he [Satan] went to wage war with the remnant of her offspring [believers], who keep the commandments of God and have the testimony of Jesus Christ.
> —REVELATION 12:4–5, 13, 17

Satan tried to kill Jesus when He was born, and failed. In Matthew 2:16 we see the devil's attempt to take Jesus' life on earth when Herod "killed all the male children who were in Bethlehem and the surrounding region, from two years old and under." When Yeshua ascended to heaven, Satan then waged war upon Israel and all God's children. Satan, the Antichrist, the demons of hell, and every evil force of the enemy are all aiming for one thing: to annihilate God's people.

The enemy knows Yeshua cannot be destroyed and that He is in heaven. So Satan's final campaign is to cause God pain by hurting His people. Any parent knows that if you really want to hurt someone, you go after his or her children. And that is exactly what the Antichrist will do. He will act according to Satan's agenda to hurt God by attacking His kids.

## THE ANTI-ANOINTING

We must not forget that the Anti-Messiah is the exact counterfeit of the true Messiah, Yeshua. Everything Satan does is false. John 8:44 says Satan "was a murderer from the beginning, and does not stand in the truth, because there is no truth in him. When he lies, he speaks from his own nature, for he is a liar and the father of lies." As the great deceiver, the only thing Satan can do is create counterfeit copies of God's original versions.

This is why we see even a counterfeit, satanic trinity in the end-times story involving a dragon (Satan), beast (Antichrist), and false prophet. (See Revelation 16:13; 19:20.) Satan, the dragon, is the counterfeit equivalent to the Father; the beastly Antichrist is supposed to imitate Jesus, the Son; and the false prophet is a false replica of the Holy Spirit. All three will work together in the last days to destroy God's people, and all three eventually will meet their eternal fate in the lake of fire.

While on earth the Anti-Messiah will be "anointed" by Satan in the same way Yeshua was anointed by the Father. This means the Antichrist will be empowered with every demonic force available. Satan, "who deceives the whole world" (Rev. 12:9), will ultimately "anoint" his son with the only real thing he can offer: deception. Yet before you begin to think that all the Antichrist will be able to do is lie, realize that he will be the manifestation of a supernatural spirit of deception that not only has duped the world for thousands of years but in the end times will also be accompanied by powerful signs and wonders. We see traces of it even now in the multitude of stories about near-death experiences. Many of these people are not believers, yet they claim to have gone to heaven, making it seem as if people don't need to profess faith in Yeshua to spend eternity in heaven.

Remember that the passage we read earlier from Daniel 8 says the Antichrist's "power shall be mighty, but not by his own power....By his cunning, he shall cause deceit to succeed under his hand" (Dan. 8:24–25). The B'rit Hadashah's counterpart to these verses, 2 Thessalonians 2, adds that the Antichrist's "coming is in accordance with the working of Satan with all power and signs and false wonders, and with all deception of unrighteousness among those who perish" (2 Thess. 2:9–10). Notice the use of the word *all* in that passage—"*all* power and signs and false wonders" and "*all* deception." This will be a full-throttle, all-out blitz attack from the forces of evil, all channeled into the Antichrist.

Just as Jesus walked in power and used signs, wonders, and healings to attest to the truth of His divinity, the Anti-Messiah will use signs and wonders to deceive people into believing he is the actual messiah. Some believe that Revelation 13:3 implies he will even be resurrected, which will cause many to conclude that he is sent from God.

Sadly, I meet many believers today who would be prime candidates to be deceived by the Antichrist's otherworldly powers. They go through life seeking one experience with God after another, one feeling or physical healing or blessing or supernatural sign. They attend conference after conference chasing only experiences instead of the truth of God. It's not wrong to seek the Lord for miracles, experiences, and healing; I desire these too. And God wants us to come to Him for everything. But there is a problem when we desire those things more than we desire Him and truth.

On the opposite end of the spectrum are those who are

drifting away from the faith or consider Christianity irrelevant to their daily lives. Church attendance fell dramatically during the COVID pandemic, with many people apparently finding church as nonessential as some local governments did. On top of that, a growing number of Americans are claiming no religious affiliation, identifying as atheist, agnostic, or nothing in particular.

Many believers have held on to the scripture that says, "Train up a child in the way he should go: and when he is old, he will not depart from it" (Prov. 22:6, KJV). Yet today many young people were not "trained up in the way they should go," so they don't know where to "return" now that they're older. During the hippie era, teens and young adults strayed from the faith, but after they got married and had children, they returned to the church. That's not happening anymore because the church is unfamiliar to many young adults.

This is exactly how so many will fall in the end times. Either they will be so desperate for the spectacular they will fall for demonic signs and wonders, or they will have so little understanding of Christianity they won't recognize truth from lies.

Scripture repeatedly warns us to stand true to the faith amid the false prophets, false teachings, and false gospels of the last days. Even today many are straying from the truth that was once and for all delivered to us by the apostles. According to one study, only a third of Americans believe Jesus is the only way to salvation,[8] and another study found that more than 60 percent of born-again Christians under the age of forty believe Jesus, Buddha, and Muhammad are all equally valid paths to salvation.[9]

Paul said if anyone preached a different gospel than the one he preached, "Let him be accursed" (Gal. 1:8). But many are preaching a gospel today that is not the one Paul preached. Paul declared a God-centered gospel that focused on the cross and demanded obedience. The false gospel that many receive today is man-centered and prosperity-focused and does not require repentance. This gospel of greasy grace and sloppy agape will not prepare us for the end times.

What's more, society has created a religion of unity and tolerance, elevating it as the highest moral ethic while demonizing the hard truths in Scripture as oppressive and outdated. As the Antichrist emerges, more and more people will receive and believe in this false gospel of political correctness and tolerance. This will apply even more when the Antichrist is surrounded by signs and wonders appearing to confirm that God has sent him.

Let's get one thing straight: Satan is not dumb. He will not make the Antichrist *look* evil. No, just as Satan sometimes "disguises himself as an angel of light" (2 Cor. 11:14), the Anti-Messiah will be anti-anointed with a covering that makes him look more appealing—in fact, more so than any other leader in history. He will not look like the devil but instead will be incredibly charismatic, compassionate, gracious, and seemingly loving. He will reach out to all humanity, show mercy to all, and reinforce his tolerance for all kinds of people. The crowds will flock around him, just as they did Jesus, because they will fall in love with his words of wisdom, his heart, his inclusiveness, and his power. Simply stated, he will seem like the Son of God.

## THE REALITY OF THE ANTICHRIST

John writes in Revelation 6: "Then I saw when the Lamb broke one of the seven seals, and I heard one of the four living creatures saying as with a voice of thunder, 'Come.' I looked, and behold, a white horse, and he who sat on it had a bow; and a crown was given to him, and he went out conquering and to conquer" (vv. 1–2, NASB). Messiah Jesus will return on a white horse (Rev. 19:11–16), but the rider of the white horse in this passage is not Yeshua. This rider is the Antichrist, a satanic imposter who will imitate the Savior. He will deceive the masses into believing he represents the highest form of godliness, but his aim is to conquer.

Behind all the lies of inclusion, peace, and one-world unity the Antichrist will have one ultimate goal: to exalt himself. His deep hatred for Jesus will reveal itself midway through the great tribulation when he removes a system of worship set up for the Lord. His pride will be on full display when he establishes a system for the world to worship him instead. Once again we turn to the Hebrew prophet Daniel's words for the description of the Antichrist, who in this passage is referred to as the "little horn":

> Out of one of them came a little horn, which grew exceedingly great toward the south, toward the east, and toward the Pleasant Land. It grew great, even to the host of heaven. And it cast down some of the host and of the stars to the ground and stamped upon them. Indeed, *he magnified himself even to the Prince of the host,* and from Him the daily sacrifice was taken away, and the place of His sanctuary was cast down. Because of rebellion, an army was given to the horn to oppose the daily sacrifice; and it cast truth to the ground. It practiced this and prospered.
> —Daniel 8:9–12, emphasis added

Before the world can exalt him, the Antichrist must remove its worship of Jesus and "cast truth to the ground" (v. 12). In this verse we see a sequence of events before the Anti-Messiah is able to "prosper" in his attempt to get the world to worship him instead of Yeshua. First he must remove the existing ways and structures involved in worshipping God. Daniel 9:27 says the Antichrist will "cause the sacrifice and the offering to cease." In addition, he will take away any reminders of God from the place of worship.

When Daniel says "the place of His sanctuary was cast down" (Dan. 8:11), I believe it is not just a literal destruction of the temple in Jerusalem but also an ideological demolition of any belief that the God of the Bible is to be honored at all, or that He even exists. It does not take much investigation to see that a removal of Judeo-Christian values is already happening. The law of our land now makes public prayer illegal in our school systems. We have removed any physical trace of the Ten Commandments from government properties. And those who attempt to worship or pray in Jesus' name at public events risk being accused of or even charged with hate crimes.

Hollywood and the news media mock God, presenting people of faith as extremist, hateful, or ignorant—and this will only get worse. Several months ago during my daily devotional, I asked the Lord if He wanted to draw my attention to any scriptures outside my standard reading. I opened the Word at random to the Book of Esther, specifically chapter 9, which says "the Jews themselves gained the mastery over those who hated them" and "struck all their enemies with the sword, killing and destroying; and they did what they pleased to those who hated them" (vv. 1, 5, NASB).

When I read that, it was like a bomb of Holy Spirit revelation went off in my mind, and I heard the Lord say to me (not audibly but in my intuition): "This is what's coming next. The world is going to start pinpointing scriptures like the one you just read where it says the Jews did whatever they wanted with their enemies to foster and bolster anti-Semitism."

Beloved, the Lord showed me three months before the Israel-Hamas War broke out that the media is going to start focusing on Jews bombing sites on their borders where they're being attacked, but they aren't going to portray the Jewish people as protecting themselves. (To hear the full prophecy from July 7, 2023, see my video "The Anchor Is Gone," beginning at the 16-minute, 8-second mark. You'll find the link in the end notes.[10]) They're going to report that Israel bombed locations where children got hurt, and the world is going to turn against the Jews once again. But this time the hatred is not going to come from just one nation as it did in the days of Nazi Germany. The whole world is going to turn against the Jews, and I believe the anti-Semitism will be even worse than it was under Hitler. We're about to see the biggest attack against Jewish people the world has ever known.

As part of this agenda, the devil is going to start highlighting scriptures, particularly those in the Torah like 1 Samuel 15:3, where the Lord commanded the Israelites to go into the territory of Amalek and "utterly destroy all that he has, and do not spare him; but put to death both man and woman, child and infant, ox and sheep, camel and donkey" (NASB). The enemy is going to put scriptures like that on television, in school systems, over the airwaves, and on the internet to breathe a hatred against the God of Israel.

It's coming, beloved one. Followers of Yeshua are about to be attacked worse than ever. A storm is brewing, and those who don't put God first—spending time with Him and getting in the Word daily—won't be able to stand when the storm gets fiercer.

After the Antichrist eliminates any worship of the true God, he will proceed to "cast truth to the ground" (Dan. 8:12) and reprogram people's minds to believe what is false—essentially to believe that what is wrong is right and what is right is wrong (Isa. 5:20). He will even brainwash people so they will believe his lies as a more advanced "truth."

Once again we see traces of this already in progress throughout our education system. From elementary schools to university campuses, students are no longer taught that God created them; in fact, such teaching can get educators fired. Instead, children learn that they have evolved from a cosmic explosion in space, which came from—well, evolutionists still haven't figured that part out, and that we are all the result of some great evolutionary phenomenon with no intelligent design behind it. Meanwhile in our courtrooms we have now cast to the ground the truth of biblical marriage between one man and one woman, and now all states must recognize marriage between members of the same sex.

The Antichrist will not be content with removing that which belongs to Jesus. He will want to take the very place of God in the hearts and minds of people. Just as the Hebrew prophets revealed this self-exaltation in the Old Testament, so did Paul in the New Testament:

> For that Day will not come unless a falling away comes first, and the man of sin is revealed, the son of destruction, who opposes and *exalts himself above all that is called God or is worshipped*, so that

he sits as God in the temple of God, showing himself as God.

                    —2 THESSALONIANS 2:3–4, EMPHASIS ADDED

After the Antichrist tears down whatever worship Jesus
would rightfully receive, he will then position himself as the
one to be worshipped. He will take God's place and demand
that people worship him.

## THE SPIRIT OF SELF-EXALTATION

Allow me to stretch your perspective a bit. Most Bible scholars
believe the Antichrist will literally sit in a third temple in
Jerusalem, based on 2 Thessalonians 2:4, or that he will
partner with the false prophet to set up an "image" of himself that people will worship, according to Revelation 13:14–15.
Many believe the "abomination of desolation" mentioned in
Matthew 24:15 will be intricately connected to people worshipping an Antichrist image in the rebuilt third temple in
Jerusalem. (See also Daniel 9:27.)

In 167 BC Antiochus Epiphanes, a Greek ruler who sought
to exalt himself so much that he named himself "god mani-
fest," raided the temple in Jerusalem, set up an altar to Zeus,
and used temple artifacts to sacrifice a pig. Jews in Yeshua's
time referred to this blatant insult as the "abomination of
desolation," and it is obvious from Daniel's and Yeshua's
words that the Anti-Messiah will do something equally
offensive. Naturally many scholars predict it will come in a
literal temple built in Jerusalem. But let me ask you a question: Where is the temple of God today?

Acts 7:48, Acts 17:24, and 1 Corinthians 3:16 all make the
same point—that God no longer dwells in a temple made by

human hands, but in the ultimate temple *He* created with His holy hands: us! Scripture says we are His temple and that Christ now dwells in our hearts (Eph. 3:17). His Holy Spirit now resides in each of us as believers. He is worshipped with the fragrance of love that emerges when our lives are poured out to Him.

Yet what is the focal point of our culture's "worship" today? Me. Me. Me! The centerpiece of Western society is self. *I deserve this. I'm good enough. I'm strong enough. I'm powerful enough. I can do this.* It's all about *me, me, me.*

Such self-worship is the very heart of Satan. It is why he was thrown out of heaven, as described in Isaiah 14:

> How are you fallen from heaven, O Lucifer, son of
> the morning! How you are cut down to the ground,
> you who weaken the nations! For you have said in
> your heart, "I will ascend into heaven, I will exalt
> my throne above the stars of God; I will sit also on
> the mount of the congregation, in the recesses of the
> north; I will ascend above the heights of the clouds,
> I will be like the Most High."
>
> —ISAIAH 14:12–14

Satan exalted himself because he wanted to receive worship rather than ascribe it to God. He wanted to take God's place.

Sound familiar?

Indeed, what the Antichrist will attempt to do in the last days has already begun. We are seeing the prophecies fulfilled today with the extreme egocentric worship in our society. Satan is taking his seat on the throne of human hearts around the world. He is taking God's place by inhabiting human hearts to such a degree that they think they are God. In our selfie-obsessed world more people than ever stand in front of their mirrors and truly see themselves as the center of the universe. With such false worship already covering the world, is it possible that the abomination of desolation Yeshua and Daniel spoke of may not only pertain to the temple in Jerusalem made of stone, but even more so to the altars of human hearts? I believe it is.

## I PLEDGE ALLEGIANCE TO...

A few years ago I dreamed that I was preaching at a church. As I was speaking God's Word in the dream, all the congregation members stood up and placed their hands upon their hearts. I was puzzled by their actions, but I continued preaching, not knowing what they were doing. Suddenly they began to recite the Pledge of Allegiance aloud, and their voices became a single roar: "I pledge allegiance to the flag of the United States of America and to the republic for which it stands..." Though I continued to speak, their voices quickly drowned out my preaching.

I was so humiliated that I left the room and found a restroom in which to hide. While in the restroom I asked the Lord, "Do I have to go back in there?"

"Yes," He replied. "Go in there and finish."

I walked back in the room, still ashamed but committed to obeying the Lord. As I approached the pulpit, however, someone stood up and said, "They don't want to listen to you anymore."

I finished the message, but I could tell the congregation was not open to hearing me, nor was it receptive to God's Word. As the dream ended, a voice spoke to me and said, "You did a good job while you were here." I remember wondering in the dream where this voice was coming from, but it continued. "Unless people are waking up in the morning and asking Me to cleanse them, the best preacher in the world won't be able to help them."

Then the dream ended. It disturbed me to the point that I was grieved for days. "What am I doing wrong?" I asked the Lord. "Why did this happen? Where am I failing as a leader that people would rise up in the middle of my message and begin to drown out Your Word with the Pledge of Allegiance? Lord, show me what I'm doing wrong. Show me what my insecurity is. Please show me where I'm failing that something like this would happen!"

I prayed like this for several days, grieving over the dream and pleading with the Lord to give me understanding. About a week later, while I was in a hotel room preparing to preach in a church, the Holy Spirit spoke to me in a crystal-clear manner: "What I showed you had nothing to do with you," He said. "What I showed you was that people's allegiance is not to Me even though they are in churches; it's to the American dream."

Beloved, I love my country. I am proud to be an American. So please don't misunderstand me; this is not meant to be unpatriotic in any way. But the truth is that being a proud patriot is different from being a follower of Jesus.

Yeshua said His kingdom was not of this world. When He asked us to follow Him, He did not set up a separate category for partial followers; it is all or nothing. To go with Him means we deny ourselves, take up our cross, and follow Him completely. Sadly, countless people sit in churches today thinking they are believers and assuming that they're following the Lord, yet in reality they are simply following the American dream.

The American dream says you can achieve anything you set your mind to. It says believe in yourself. It says if you can dream it, you can achieve it. I love my country, but the American dream today that many Christians live for is all about serving themselves—about worshipping at the altar of "me." This is exactly the opposite of what Jesus called us to do if we want to follow Him.

Satan loves the gospel of me. It is exactly what the Antichrist will be pushing in the end times. But until then, he loves the fact that much of America—including many in the church— has already succumbed to this self-worshipping gospel. When we follow the American dream more than God's Word, it makes us prime candidates to be deceived by the great deceiver. And the more of us he can fool, the easier his job will be in the last days when he implements a global system that will literally and permanently mark who is deceived.

## THE MARK OF THE BEAST

Two places in the Book of Revelation describe what we call "the mark of the beast." Remember, the beast is simply another name for the Antichrist.

> He causes all, both small and great, both rich and poor, both free and slave, to receive a mark on their right hand or on their forehead, so that no one may buy or sell, except he who has the mark or the name of the beast or the number of his name. Here is a call for wisdom: Let him who has understanding

calculate the number of the beast. It is the number
of a man. His number is six hundred and sixty-six.
—REVELATION 13:16–18

A third angel followed them, saying with a loud
voice, "If anyone worships the beast and his image
and receives his mark on his forehead or on his hand,
he also shall drink of the wine of the wrath of God,
which is poured out in full strength into the cup of
His anger. He shall be tormented with fire and brimstone in the presence of the holy angels and in the
presence of the Lamb. The smoke of their torment
will ascend forever and ever. They have no rest day
or night, who worship the beast and his image and
whoever receives the mark of his name."
—REVELATION 14:9–11

This is no small thing. The mark of the beast will literally signify those who will spend eternity with Satan in the
lake of fire. For those who refuse to take the mark, life will
be extremely difficult—that is, if they aren't already killed
for not taking the mark in the first place. Just as Jews in
Nazi Germany often were killed for not wearing a Jewish
star or for refusing to salute Adolf Hitler and the Nazi Party,
so it will be for believers who do not have the mark of the
beast. Yet as we will see in the next chapter, I believe God
will give supernatural grace and provision for those who
refuse to receive the mark and thus will be unable to take
part in the global economic system during the Antichrist's
reign. Regardless of how costly taking the mark is on earth,
it cannot compare to the price of eternal damnation.

In recent generations many have speculated that the mark

of the beast could be a computer chip placed under the skin for numerical identification. The technology is already available to create scannable implants that can be used for everything from purchasing products to unlocking doors to starting a vehicle.[19] So what was once an imaginative yet eerie idea is now reality.

People have speculated about the mark of the beast for centuries, and I do not intend to split hairs over what exactly it will be like. Instead I want to highlight how once again Satan can do nothing but counterfeit what the Lord created—yes, even when it comes to the mark of the beast.

In the Book of D'varim (Deuteronomy) the Lord instructed the children of Israel on how they should keep His words of life close to them:

> These words, which I am commanding you today, shall be in your heart....You shall bind them as a sign on your hand, and they shall be as frontlets between your eyes.
>
> —DEUTERONOMY 6:6, 8

Elsewhere in the Torah God gave the same instructions, always referring to His Law being impressed not just on their hearts and in their minds but upon their physical bodies as well. In obedience to God's commands the children of Israel began wearing tefillin, or phylacteries (Exod. 13:16; Matt. 23:5)—small boxes that contained portions of the Torah and were bound around the hand or arm and around the head, right between the eyes. Every Jew understood the symbolism of this act: You were binding God's Word to your mind, and from the mind and thoughts came actions, expressed by the arm or hand. Scripture says a man acts based upon what he thinks (Prov. 23:7). God wants His truth to be so ingrained in our thoughts that our actions reflect it, so we can walk in His blessing.

Do you think it is mere coincidence that the mark of the beast will be placed on the forehead or the hand? I believe that Satan, through the Antichrist's global system, will present a counterfeit "law" and thought structure that will influence people's minds then become seared into their hearts and expressed through the actions of their hands.

## A COUNTERFEIT REALITY

This is not some far-off future event. Most people don't have computer chips placed under their skin to pay for goods and services yet—though the technology exists[12]—but I believe many are receiving the mark of the beast in a spiritual sense. They have exchanged God's truth in their hearts and minds for Satan's counterfeit reality.

Today we marvel at the benefits of the personal computer and how it has advanced society. But for all the many wonderful things computer technology has brought, it has also ushered in an era of unparalleled addictions of every kind—from social media to pornography to online gambling to simple screen time. Studies show that computers have shifted the way humans interact with one another. Social media in particular has been found to have a negative neurological impact on language development and processing emotional cues.[13] Simply put, computers have changed the way we think and rewired our brains.

Add to that the emergence of artificial intelligence (AI). For any good it may bring, we're just beginning to see its implicit dangers and even the existential threat it poses.[14]

Before long, anyone will, at the click of a button, be able to take your image and make you say anything they want—the video will look and sound exactly like you. One of the premier leaders of artificial intelligence, Elon Musk, is terrified of its capability, saying, "AI is more dangerous than, say, mismanaged aircraft design...or bad car production, in the sense that it...has the potential...of civilization destruction."[15]

I think the danger of AI may be greater than the threat of nuclear warheads. Mark my words. AI is capable of vastly more than almost anyone knows, and its rate of improvement is exponential. Effectively, we are building progressively greater intelligence, and an ever-increasing percentage of it is not human. Eventually humans will represent a very small percentage of intelligence. Please hear me: I am not against computers or smartphones or technological advancement, nor am I lobbying for a return to the "good ole days" of telegrams and rotary phones. But I find it fascinating how computers—in all their shapes, sizes, and speeds—are able to rewire people's thought processes, emotions, intellect, personalities, and cognitive abilities like few other things. A computer can literally reshape someone from the inside out!

Years ago I read the story of how Steve Jobs and Steve Wozniak, cofounders of Apple Computer, priced their first personal computer for $666.66. Obviously, much has been made of the link between this price and the biblical number of the beast, 666 (Rev. 13:18). More than once Apple's founders have claimed they did not know about the satanic association but had simply marked up the retail price to cover their manufacturing costs of $500—and they liked the eye-catching, marketing aspect of $666.66.[16]

Whether Jobs and Wozniak were aware of the connection

to the mark of the beast makes little difference. The product category they helped to launch is having a profound spiritual impact upon humanity at this time. Satan is using technology and the Internet to reprogram mankind. The mind represents the gateway (there's another "coincidental" computer-company connection!) to the soul. Through the computer Satan has drawn people into a pseudo-reality, a world full of darkness in which you can lose your identity and fulfill every sexual fantasy imaginable.

While the Lord commanded His people to bind tefillin between the frontals of their eyes and upon their arm or hand to remind them of His law of light, Satan likewise has bound the computer around the minds of individuals so that their actions reflect his darkness. Just as the Lord tried to reprogram mankind with His truth (the Law), the enemy is trying to reprogram mankind with a personal computer, one of which originally sold for $666. (See Revelation 13:18.)

In a spiritual sense the mark of the beast is simply taking the mind of the enemy and acting out of that paradigm. It is taking the deception by which the Anti-Messiah will rule—including the false American dream and the false gospel of self-exaltation—and ingesting that into our lifestyle to such a degree that our motives, goals, actions, and vision for life are all based upon that deceptive reality.

In the future receiving the mark of the beast almost certainly will be a physical act. The technology already exists, and it's conceivable that someone could say the way to solve identity theft or any number of other cybercrimes is by having people identify themselves with a chip implanted under their skin. There are already businesses that no longer accept cash; it's not such a leap to imagine a world that requires people to have a biochip with all their information in order to access the economic or healthcare system, or even to travel. This may have seemed farfetched a few years ago, but after the COVID pandemic, I think it's easy to see that we've already been primed for this kind of global shift.

Yet I don't believe receiving the mark of the beast will be solely a physical undertaking. As I said previously, it will also involve receiving Satan's false reality as truth. We must each ask ourselves today, "How much of this world am I really taking in?" Remember, Satan is currently the "ruler of this world" (John 14:30). So how much domain is he establishing in our thoughts? Are we allowing the false reality of the American dream to shape how we live by serving ourselves and building a bigger and better kingdom for ourselves? Or are we dying to "self" daily, submitting ourselves to the Father just as Jesus did, and exalting Him?

Satan wants us to exalt ourselves just as he forever exalts himself; Jesus asks us to die to ourselves. The difference is as vast as life is from death. Yeshua said, "Whoever wants to save their life will lose it, but whoever loses their life for me will find it" (Matt. 16:25, NIV). Today Satan is using false religions and false gospels—yes, even within the church—to deceive people on the path to eternal death. He has infiltrated Christianity by getting people to think they are following Jesus by sitting in a pew each Sunday, dropping a few dollars in the offering plate, and being entertained by a nice church service. Church leaders aren't helping when they give people cappuccinos in the pew, tell them God just wants them to feel good about themselves, and ensure that they get them out in an hour—yet rarely preach the cross of Christ or teach about holiness and obedience.

This is all part of Satan's big delusion. It is a false religion running rampant in today's churches—a false religion that is all about "me" and has little to do with God. A gospel of political correctness and peace at all costs—one that demands no sacrifice or obedience—is not the gospel Yeshua taught, nor is it the one delivered to us through the original apostles. There is a reason Jesus said so often, "Don't be deceived." His way is straight and narrow (Matt. 7:14). It involves a cross of self-denial, not a throne of self-exaltation. Yet ultimately it leads to life and not death.

## ENDING THE DEVIL'S DYNASTY

Satan's campaign of deception will be successful. The Antichrist will institute a global system of worship within a false religion designed to exalt himself. This false religion may not be a formal religion but perhaps a state of mind and heart that the world at large adopts. Many will fall prey to this system, taking the mark of the beast, and many believers will succumb to the spiritual pressures of the day and fall away from their faith, just as Yeshua warned. (See Matthew 24:10, 24.) And for a season before the Lord returns, the forces of evil will appear to win as the devil establishes what will seem like the greatest, most powerful dynasty in history.

But none of this changes the fact that God is still in control and will continue to be during every moment of the end times. Not one thing will happen outside His reach. So before we go further into our look at the Book of Revelation, which includes many other elements that appear frightening, heavy, and even hopeless, it is worth reminding ourselves how this story ends. In particular, it helps to keep in mind what ultimately happens to Satan, the Antichrist, the false prophet, and every force of evil that will seem to have such victory upon earth during this time.

For that ending we can turn to the Hebrew prophets, who received revelation of this more than twenty-seven hundred years ago. Remember how we read Daniel's account earlier:

> In the latter time of their kingdom, when the trans-
> gressors have reached their limit, a king will arise....
> He shall also rise up against the Prince of princes; but
> he shall be broken, not by human hands.
>                                                —DANIEL 8:23, 25

In those verses from Daniel 8 we receive our first clue about how the Anti-Messiah will be brought down and Satan's kingdom demolished. It will not be by human power but by a supernatural force. Isaiah expands on this by giving us one of the Bible's most detailed accounts of Satan's past and future fall, part of which we looked at earlier in this chapter:

> How are you fallen from heaven, O Lucifer, son of the
> morning! How you are cut down to the ground, you
> who weaken the nations! For you have said in your
> heart, "I will ascend into heaven, I will exalt my throne
> above the stars of God; I will sit also on the mount of
> the congregation, in the recesses of the north; I will
> ascend above the heights of the clouds, I will be like
> the Most High." Yet you shall be brought down to Hell,
> to the sides of the pit. Those who see you shall stare at
> you and ponder over you: "Is this the man who made
> the earth to tremble and shook kingdoms, who made

the world as a wilderness and destroyed its cities, who
did not open the house of his prisoners?"

—Isaiah 14:12–17

The first part of Isaiah's description here can be seen
entirely as the fall of Lucifer (another name for Satan) in the
past. The prophet Ezekiel affirmed that long before the creation of man, Satan, or Lucifer, was an anointed cherub "full
of wisdom and perfect in beauty" (Ezek. 28:12), but because
of his attempted self-exaltation he was "cast…to the ground"
(Ezek. 28:17; see also vv. 11, 13–16, 18–19). Because Satan
wanted to be worshipped like God and tried to "exalt [his]
throne above the stars of God" (Isa. 14:13), the Lord cast him
out of His presence.

Jesus affirmed Isaiah's and Ezekiel's accounts of a fallen
Satan. While talking to His disciples, He said, "I saw Satan as
lightning fall from heaven" (Luke 10:18). Not only was Yeshua
there when the devil was cast down from heaven to earth
ages before, but He was very much part of the process! How
remarkable is that! And how affirming is it that once again
the Hebrew Bible and New Testament line up perfectly.

Yet there is still more to be gleaned from Isaiah 14. We
read that Lucifer "shook kingdoms…made the world as
a wilderness and destroyed its cities" (vv. 16–17). Again,
Satan's campaign to "weaken the nations" (v. 12) will succeed. Earth's greatest kingdoms and leaders will be rendered
powerless under the Antichrist's authority.

Ultimately, however, we know by Isaiah's account that
Satan and the Antichrist will "be brought down to Hell, to
the sides of the pit" (v. 15). So how will Satan and his min-
ions so quickly go from ruling the world with unprecedented

authority to being looked down upon while he is in the pit of hell as if a beast in a cage?

To answer this we can again turn to the New Testament. In Paul's letter to the Thessalonians, he explains how the end of the Antichrist's grand assault will be anything but spectacular:

> Then the lawless one will be revealed, whom the Lord will consume with the breath of His mouth, and destroy with the brightness of His presence.
> —2 THESSALONIANS 2:8

Once Yeshua HaMashiach shows up, the one trying to mimic him will be toast. Satan's great pretender, who will have spent the last seven years duping the world into believing he is the son of God, will literally be destroyed at first sight. No big fight. No climactic showdown. No heated exchange of words followed by an epic struggle as if this were a movie.

No. Instead, the very light and goodness of Jesus' presence will be in such contrast to the Antichrist's wickedness that he will be dispelled instantaneously. Like human bodies turned to ashes from a nuclear explosion, the Antichrist will be destroyed in a flash by Jesus simply showing up and breathing. Tell me, who is the truly powerful one now?

*Hallelujah!*

As bad as things may seem in this world, and as difficult as life may get for believers living in the end times during the rise of the Antichrist, Yeshua will keep us. Our hope lies in the Savior who promises to protect us. Yeshua HaMashiach *will* return with unimaginable power and authority. When He does, every opposing force—including Satan, the enemy of mankind throughout history—will amount to nothing.

# CHAPTER 4

# GOD'S WRATH

As THE ANTI-MESSIAH rises to power, he will expose himself as the most evil, satanically empowered man to ever walk on earth. Though the nations of the world initially will celebrate this mysterious "man of peace" and embrace him as the heaven-sent savior, they eventually will regret the day he was given power. His actions and pure cruelty will usher in an era of unprecedented tribulation throughout the world.

Yet what the Antichrist and Satan unleash in their limited power pales in comparison to the righteous judgments God will use to begin to cleanse the world of its filth of sin and evil. In fact, the earth and its inhabitants will not have encountered God's wrath with such force since the days of Noah and the flood. But this time the earth will not be destroyed by mere water. This time God's full measure of cleansing judgment will be poured out in twenty-one portions, each building upon the previous one in intensity and destruction.

These twenty-one judgments are described in the Book of Revelation and divided into three main categories as they relate to being distributed upon the earth: seven seals, seven trumpets, and seven bowls. The seventh seal introduces the first of the seven trumpets, and likewise the seventh trumpet announces the arrival of the first bowl. (Don't worry if you feel a little overwhelmed by the details of this section; stick with your reading, and I'm confident you will absorb the main points.) In general, each judgment gets progressively worse as the tribulation continues. Some are easy to understand, such as global famine or darkness; others are harder to comprehend and may mean something we have yet to figure out, such as how a third of all the world's ships will be destroyed at once.

We must remember that Bible prophecy is rarely fulfilled the exact way people expect. This was the case before and during Jesus' time, and it will continue to be so upon His return. For example, almost five hundred years prior to Yeshua's arrival on earth the prophet Malachi issued the word of the Lord: "See, I will send you Elijah the prophet before the coming of the great and dreaded day of the Lord" (Mal. 4:5). In Matthew 11, however, Jesus publicly identified John the Baptist as "Elijah, who is to come" (v. 14). Others during Jesus' ministry thought He might be Elijah (Matt. 16:14).

Does this mean the prophecy was not fulfilled? Not quite. Malachi's words may not have come to pass in a literal sense, but they were fulfilled in a spiritual sense, which is what was intended. John was indeed the forerunner for the Lord's arrival, and the prophecy will be fulfilled yet again upon the true Day of the Lord.

In the same way, many of the judgments John speaks of in the Book of Revelation may come to pass in what we would understand to be a literal fulfillment while others may not. Only God knows. The point is that it remains possible that some of these plagues will occur in a way that is different from what we are expecting. Biblical history proves that even the most educated prophetic scholars can miss a prophecy's meaning and fulfillment, and it is very likely that during the season of the Lord's return—including the time of God's wrath unleashed—some things will happen differently than we thought they might.

Before we address the significance of this season of God's full wrath and, specifically, what it means for believers, let's briefly look at each of these seals, trumpets, and bowls in the order in which they will be released and examine what each judgment will involve. And remember, if some of these do not make sense or sound confusing to you, don't give up. Keep reading!

## SEVEN SEALS

Revelation 6 describes six of the seven seals that will be released as judgments upon the earth. The first four of these seven are often referred to as the four horsemen of the Apocalypse, as the apostle John's description of each features figurative horses with riders bent on bringing widespread damage.

### The Antichrist (Rev. 6:2)

Upon the first horse, which is white, rides the Antichrist. Once again Satan can do nothing but counterfeit God's original—thus the white horse is the same color as the horse Jesus will ride upon His return. It is also interesting to note that the Antichrist will come with a bow yet no arrows, signifying that he will arrive seemingly bent on bringing peace and that he is a false Christ. Because of the Anti-Messiah's deceptive promises of peace and people "crowning" him with authority, we will be able to discern the beginning of the tribulation by the fulfillment of this first seal.

## War and murder (Rev. 6:4)

Although the Antichrist will at first win people over with diplomacy and talks of peace, war eventually will mark his reign—particularly during the last half of the tribulation. Upon the second seal's release, the earth's murder rate will skyrocket, as the second horseman will have the power to "take peace from the earth, causing people to kill one another" (v. 4).

## Famine (Rev. 6:5–6)

The scales of the world's economy will be tipped upon this seal's release, prompting worldwide famine and food shortages, exemplified by the fact that two pounds of wheat will cost almost seventy-five dollars. Interestingly enough, however, luxuries such as oil and wine will still be present, indicating a huge disparity between the rich and poor. In modern times we have seen a country's economic collapse spark such famine and financial disparity. When the former Soviet Union's economy collapsed in 1991, for example, bread prices shot up more than 600 percent.[1] Just a few years later Russia boasted an unusual number of the world's richest individuals while the majority of its citizens lived paycheck to paycheck.[2] In the end times such dramatic shifts will pave the way for even more upheaval.

## Death (Rev. 6:8)

The death toll will escalate with the fourth seal, by which one-fourth of the world's population will die as a result of starvation, war and violence, disease, attacks by animals and beasts, or natural causes.

## Persecution of the saints (Rev. 6:9–11)

Most people interpret these verses to be specific to believers who were martyred *in the past*. However, this fifth seal also represents those who are yet to die for their faith during the difficult tribulation years. More believers have died for their faith in the past one hundred years than in all other centuries combined, yet in the tribulation we can expect martyrdom to reach unprecedented levels.[3]

As perhaps a precursor to that time, we are seeing another, though far less serious, form of persecution of the saints even now. Nearly half of all evangelical leaders in the United States report that they have been "canceled" by being disinvited, blacklisted, or excluded based on their beliefs.[4] The same is happening to believers in other spheres. Educators who profess Christian values report being denied tenure and promotions. Scientists who believe in intelligent design over the randomness of the big bang theory have had similar experiences, with some saying they're not being hired at all. Perhaps this is why a survey by *The Harvard Crimson* found that less than 1 percent of Harvard's faculty is made up of "very conservative" professors.[5]

Yet none of this should come as a surprise. Yeshua said in Matthew 24, "You will be hated by all nations for My name's sake" (v. 9). That's where we're headed, and the early signs are evident.

## Cosmic and ecological disaster (Rev. 6:12–17)

Up to this point in the tribulation most of the earth's deaths can be attributed to earthbound causes. By some reports, our planet has heated up by double-digit degrees Fahrenheit over the last century, causing ice sheets in Greenland and Antarctica to shrink, glaciers around the world to retreat, snow cover to decrease, and the global sea level to rise.[6] I realize many question whether the climate is truly changing. Whatever the cause, in recent years we have seen bigger, longer-lasting wildfires, more frequent and catastrophic hurricanes, heavy rains and flooding, and record-high temperatures, with 2023 having been the warmest year since global recordkeeping began in 1850.[7]

By the sixth seal, however, the disorder of the sun, moon, and stars will throw the entire earth into chaos, causing such massive earthquakes and shifts in the planet's weather and landscape that people everywhere will try to hide in caves (some for safety and others to attempt suicide). Noteworthy in these verses is that people will recognize that these are judgments sent by God, yet Scripture gives no indication whether their hearts will soften.

**Silence and fear (Rev. 8:1)**

By the end of the sixth seal everyone on earth (aside from discerning believers and Satan's agents) will be panic-stricken and gripped with fear, with many wishing they could die. So when the seventh seal brings a brief period of respite, I wonder if people will think the worst is over or if their fear will grow. After all, is there anything more terrifying than the silence before the storm?

## SEVEN TRUMPETS

Revelation 8 and 9 depict most of the seven trumpets, which will be blown from heaven by seven angels. Their piercing blasts will sound the alarm of further judgment from God throughout the earth.

## Hail, fire, and blood (Rev. 8:7)

Upon the first trumpet being blown, a mixture of hail and bloody fire will fall upon the earth, completely burning up all the grass on the planet, along with one-third of the trees. In 1888 a hailstorm killed 246 people in Moradabad, India, and nearby Bareilly, marking history's deadliest hailstorm.[8] Considered the largest wildfire in history, the Black Friday Bushfire of 1939 burned through a staggering five million acres (seventy-eight hundred square miles) of Australia's Victoria State, killing seventy-one people and destroying eleven hundred homes and other structures.[9] In the United States, wildfires in California came close to beating that record in 2020, burning more than four million acres across the state.[10] We can be assured the hail, fire, and blood falling from the sky during this first trumpet judgment will claim even more lives and cause far more destruction.

## Oceanic disaster (Rev. 8:8–9)

When a massive meteor, volcano, or fiery mountain is cast into the ocean after the second trumpet, one-third of the seas' water will be turned to blood, killing a third of all marine life and destroying a third of the world's ships. How exactly this will happen is a mystery; indeed it is difficult to imagine how something falling into the ocean will logistically be able to wreck one-third of all the earth's ships. We can only speculate what this will look like if it occurs in a literal way, and it also remains entirely possible that this calamity could happen in a spiritual sense.

But with changing ocean conditions, what is possible from a natural standpoint is largely unknown. In recent decades, the world's oceans have been experiencing unprecedented warming, with a growing number reaching heat levels high enough not only to kill marine life and birds but also to produce cyclones and hurricanes strong enough to cause widespread devastation. As the ocean waters warm, coral reefs in the Florida Keys also have been losing their color, a phenomenon known as coral bleaching, and 95 percent of the kelp off the Northern California coast has died. Besides the oceans becoming more acidic and inhospitable to some marine life, a 2023 study found that more than half of the world's oceans have shifted in color from blue to a greener hue, likely due to changing organisms in the water.[11]

Whether the disaster in verses 8 and 9 is physical or spiritual, those living during the tribulation will witness an unsurpassed oceanic disaster.

### Toxic water (Rev. 8:10–11)

Another falling meteor will poison the earth's freshwater supplies upon the third trumpet, causing many people to die.

### Darkening (Rev. 8:12–13)

At sound of the fourth trumpet, the cosmos will be darkened by one-third, affecting both night and day and thus the planet's vegetation and crop supplies.

### Demonic "locusts" (Rev. 9:1–11)

Before we talk about the strange creatures released upon the earth at the blowing of the fifth trumpet, it is important to understand that what John saw cannot adequately be described using today's language, because what he saw was not of this world. Six times in the Book of Revelation John uses the phrase "something like" to describe what he saw because there is nothing in this realm exactly like it. That is particularly true here when he describes the fifth trumpet's release of one of the tribulation's most terrifying swarms. When another massive meteor hits the earth, unimaginable creatures—a blend of locusts, scorpions, horses, lions, and humans—will come out of its crater to torment people everywhere. Life will be so miserable that even those who attempt suicide will be unsuccessful (v. 6). Those who "have the seal of God on their foreheads," however, will be spared this demonic assault (v. 4).

### Deadly army and plagues (Rev. 9:13–21)

At the sixth trumpet's sounding, a third of all people on earth will be killed by a massive otherworldly army (two hundred million strong!) and horrific plagues.

### Seven angels with the seven bowls of wrath (Rev. 11:15–19; 15:1–8)

Much like the seventh seal, the seventh trumpet will release the "contents" of the next category of judgments—which in this case is the greatest level of God's wrath ever unleashed upon earth. It's definitely not good news for those still remaining, but for those who trust in the Lord, it is a completely different story (as we will soon see).

## SEVEN BOWLS

Imagine a large container of liquid being poured onto a table, spreading out over the tabletop, running to every corner and side, and eventually falling over the table's edges. If you can picture this, then you can get a sense of how these final seven judgments, as described in Revelation 16, will be emptied out and quickly dispersed over the entire surface of the earth.

### Sores (Rev. 16:2)

Those who received the mark of the beast and worshipped the Antichrist will be infested with painful sores when the first bowl is poured out. Today the World Health Organization reports that 67 percent of the world's population under the age of fifty is infected with the herpes simplex virus type 1 (HSV-1).[12] Although that number sounds apocalyptic in its global reach, consider that herpes is a manageable disease mostly involving a few painful blisters or ulcers. The type of sores unleashed by this first bowl of wrath will cause far more pain and affect an even greater percentage of the remaining population.

### Marine life killed (Rev. 16:3)

The second bowl will destroy all sea creatures because the sea will be turned to blood.

### Water turned to blood (Rev. 16:3–7)

Whereas the third trumpet will make the earth's freshwater supply toxic, this third bowl will literally turn every remaining body of water into blood.

### Scorching (Rev. 16:8–9)

Already covered with sores, the peoples of the earth will then be scorched by the sun's direct rays upon the outpouring of the fourth bowl. As worried as some are today about depleting the ozone layer and global warming, one can hardly imagine what it will be like when there is no filter in the atmosphere to protect humankind from the direct rays of the sun.

## Darkness and pain (Rev. 16:10–11)

The fifth bowl once again will target those who pledge their allegiance to the Antichrist. This time they will live in complete darkness while the pain of their sores—and of their mere existence, for that matter—will increase. Despite this, their hearts will still be filled with hatred toward God.

## Euphrates dries up (Rev. 16:12–14)

However one interprets these verses, it is clear that the sixth bowl will create a channel for the Antichrist armies to move into position for the final world war at Armageddon. What makes this war unlike any other in history is that its armies will be both flesh-and-blood soldiers and supernatural forces. Demons and unclean spirits will be released through Satan, the Antichrist, and the false prophet to empower those fighting against Jesus.

## Great earthquake and hail (Rev. 16:17–21)

The last judgment unleashed before the climactic end-times showdown at Armageddon will be the most massive earthquake ever experienced on earth. Every city except Jerusalem and Babylon will be leveled, as will the mountains of the earth. Whatever is left standing after the earthquake likely will be destroyed by the hundred-pound hail that follows.

## REMEMBERING THE BIG PICTURE

Why? Why such extensive damage and destruction? Why such an elaborate strategy to break down the world? Is all this really necessary? Why will God go through so much trouble to destroy His own creation?

We may ask questions like these after seeing such a long list of terrifying judgments. In fact, it's easy to wonder how a loving God could plan something we think is so over the top in terms of pain, destruction, and utter ruin. Before we tackle this difficult issue, we must first address the deeper reason behind God's wrath being unleashed in the first place. When we look only at God's end-times judgments and do not consider the bigger picture as God sees it, we can easily be confused or even offended by His end-times plan. But when we discover more about His heart and character, it becomes easier to understand His actions and even find answers for our deeper questions. By focusing first on the *who* of this equation—God—we eventually will discover more about the what, why, when, where, and how of the tribulation.

So why would a *loving* God unleash such awesome wrath upon His own creation? To answer this, we must keep in mind two of God's primary attributes: His mercy and His justice. Sin is what spoiled God's creation, yet He has tolerated sin's presence on earth since the fall of Adam and Eve. This does not change how God feels about sin; it is still abhorrent to Him. Whereas God is life, sin is death; it pollutes and destroys what He created perfect.

Yet because of God's supreme love for mankind, He has been patient in not bringing about justice. Direct justice would be for Him to immediately destroy the earth and its inhabitants for their sinful condition. After all, we know "the wages of sin is death"—this is its price tag (Rom. 6:23). Yet God loves people so much that He has repeatedly given them opportunity to renounce sin and turn to Him in repentance so they can be saved. Peter communicated this when he spoke about the delay of Jesus' return:

> Beloved, do not be ignorant of this one thing, that with the Lord one day is as a thousand years, and a thousand years as one day. The Lord is not slow concerning His promise, as some count slowness. But He is patient with us, because *He does not want any to perish, but all to come to repentance.*
>
> —2 PETER 3:8–9, EMPHASIS ADDED

Peter was saying that Yeshua has not yet returned because He is waiting for others to come to Him. The Lord is patient in His return because He doesn't want to destroy people. He has given humanity much time to turn to Him so that He doesn't have to extinguish them. His heart is not to destroy but to save. As Luke 9:56 says, "For the Son of Man did not come to destroy men's lives but to save them."

The Lord longs to completely remove the stain of sin from this world so that we can enjoy a perfect existence with Him. Because of His mercy and His love for you and me, He sent His Son to deliver us from sin's destruction. For more than two thousand years His message of salvation has gone out, calling for mankind to repent and return to Him, to be forgiven, and to be spared from the just punishment for sin. Although sin's power on earth was overcome when Jesus died on the cross, this does not mean the *effects* of sin were removed. We see these effects daily on display in the increasing evil that permeates and defiles this world, and this evil will continue to expand to unprecedented levels in the last days.

In chapter 1 we examined how Jesus compared the rampant sin of the end times to the days of Noah and Lot. We also saw how sin will become so ever-present and cause

such destruction on earth that God will have no choice—
because of justice itself—but to cleanse the planet through
His judgments and start over with a new creation, just as He
did with the flood in Noah's day. That means by the time
God's judgments and wrath fall upon the earth through the
seven seals, seven trumpets, and seven bowls, all those who
would be willing to respond to His merciful call will have
already done so. Those who remain on earth will have, sadly
enough, chosen to reject God's invitation and to willingly
cling to sin. (See 2 Timothy 3:2–5.)

This is a crucial point to understand when answering the
question of how a loving God could bring about such seemingly "harsh" judgment. In truth, His response will not be
harsh, unfair, or excessive; it will be completely necessary
and just, given the extreme sin destroying His once-sinless
creation. God shows His mercy, not His cruelty, in that He
has waited as long as He has to destroy sin and all those who
love it.

Remember, Peter said this when he explained that Jesus
has already been patient—by waiting now more than two
thousand years—because "He does not want any to perish"
(2 Pet. 3:9).

## Mercy Revealed

In light of God's patient mercy the "plagues" of His judgments in the last days take on new meaning, don't they?
I believe the seals, trumpets, and bowls of His wrath will
become increasingly worse because the Lord actually wants
people to turn to Him when these plagues begin to fall. The
Lord desires that when these calamities take place, humankind will respond by turning to Him and being saved. By the

time the bowls of wrath are poured out, again, all those who could have turned to Him will have already done so—and all that will be left to pour out is His full wrath, to expedite the process of cleansing the earth. Even in His just wrath, then, the Lord displays His heart of mercy for mankind.

One of the Torah's most powerful and profound revelations of God highlights this twofold nature of His mercy and justice. Moses asked God to show him His glory, and the Lord responded by promising, "I will make all My goodness pass before you, and I will proclaim the name of the LORD before you. I will be gracious to whom I will be gracious and will show mercy on whom I will show mercy" (Exod. 33:19). Immediately we see that God's glory—which will cover the earth when Jesus returns—is permeated with His goodness and mercy. In the next chapter of Exodus God reveals this even more fully when Moses experiences His glory up close.

> The LORD passed by before him, and proclaimed, "The LORD, the LORD God, *merciful* and *gracious*, slow to anger, and abounding in *goodness* and truth, keeping mercy for thousands, *forgiving iniquity* and transgression and sin, but who will by no means clear the guilty, visiting the iniquity of fathers on the children and on the children's children, to the third and the fourth generation."
> —EXODUS 34:6–7, EMPHASIS ADDED

What is the very first characteristic the Lord reveals to explain to Moses who He is? His mercy! "The LORD, the LORD God, merciful and gracious" (v. 6). But He is also just ("who will by no means clear the guilty," v. 7). Indeed His justice ensures that those who revel in their sin will feel its effects "to the third and the fourth generation" (v. 7).

He is both merciful *and* just. What He showed Moses in the cleft of the rock is what He wants to reveal to people today—namely that He is first full of mercy! He has been "merciful...gracious, [and] slow to anger" since before creation, and He will continue to be that way through the seemingly "extreme" events surrounding His judgments and wrath. The Lord does not change (Mal. 3:6). The God of the Hebrew Bible is the same God today, and He will be the same God in the last days. Hallelujah!

CHAPTER 5

# THE RAPTURE

THERE IS NO greater source to know God than the Bible. It is His written, living Word that reveals Him to us. Through the Bible we discover the truth of who God is and what He is like. And yet countless believers start out on the wrong foot in their pursuit to know God because of the way they view the Bible. Many see God's Word as two separate books—the Old Testament and the New Testament—and this often affects how they view God, as if He changes from one account to the other. They may not admit this out loud, but they think it when they characterize Him as mostly judgmental in the Old Testament and mostly loving in the New Testament. I have struggled with this at times, and I know most believers have as well.

God is the same in the Old Testament as in the New Testament. But we can miss this—and distort our view of God—when we fail to see the Bible as one complete book. Some of you reading this book have had a new revelation about the Old Testament, or the Tanakh, and that is wonderful. But did you also know that we cannot fully understand the B'rit Hadashah, or the New Testament, if we do not read it through the lens of the Tanakh?

In other words, we must understand the New Testament in light of the Old Testament. We cannot interpret the New Testament in a vacuum or treat the Bible as if it begins with Matthew 1. The New Testament was meant to be viewed through the lens of the Old Testament.

In addition, the B'rit Hadashah was never written to be detached from the Tanakh. If we want to interpret the Bible correctly, then we must interpret it as a whole, starting with Genesis and continuing all the way through the last chapter of Revelation. This is why Jesus frequently quoted from the Tanakh, validating its authenticity as the Word of God. The apostles and early church writers constantly referenced the Hebrew prophets of the Old Testament for the same reason.

For example, the Book of Matthew begins with a genealogy of Yeshua, traced all the way back to Abraham. Matthew's genealogy is not just a long, boring list of names; those names are the actual, historic links between the Old and New Testaments. In God's eyes they are one book— His written Word, the Old and New Testament, stitched together. And what is the main thread that binds them? Yeshua HaMashiach. He even said in John 5:46, "For if you believed Moses, you would believe Me, for he wrote of Me."

## The Lamb of God

The foundational truth of the Bible's unity is essential to remember as we continue our study of the end times. As has been stated, the Book of Revelation is the greatest body of literature we have on the end times. But to study it correctly, we must see it through the complete lens of the Old Testament. And possibly nothing confirms this principle more in the Book of Revelation than how Jesus is referred to most often in that book.

Did you know that Yeshua is called the "Lamb of God" twenty-nine times in Revelation? That is remarkable considering there are only twenty-two chapters in the book! In Revelation 5:6, for example, John says he "saw a Lamb in the

midst of the throne…standing as though it had been slain."
Only two verses later, he says those in the throne room "fell
down before the Lamb" (v. 8), only to be joined by countless
voices crying out, "Worthy is the Lamb who was slain" (v. 12)
and, "To Him who sits on the throne and to the Lamb be
blessing and honor and glory and power, forever and ever!"
(v. 13). Regarding Armageddon, John says the armies of the
world "will wage war with the Lamb, but the Lamb will
overcome them, for He is Lord of lords and King of kings"
(Rev. 17:14). And in Revelation 21:23 the New Jerusalem is
described as a place where there is no need for sunlight or
moonlight because "its lamp is the Lamb."

But why is Jesus called this so often? Why the *Lamb* of
God? Why not the mighty horse of God? Or the powerful
bear of God? At the very least, why not the great Lion of
Judah, which He is also called in Revelation? Lions and bears
and horses are much more powerful than lambs, aren't they?

We know for certain that when Jesus returns, He will not
be coming as some soft, fuzzy figure—certainly not lamb-
like. He will return with more power than this world has
ever seen—enough that the Antichrist, as we saw in the last
chapter, will be destroyed by the mere light and breath of
Jesus' presence!

So again, why a lamb? This is not some small, insignificant
question. It is at the core of everything we study in this book.
I believe the answer to this question reveals the truth not
only about the last days and why they must happen as they
will, but also about God's character, His love for the world,
and even the bigger picture of why He created the world—
and us—in the first place. Ultimately I believe the answer
to why Yeshua is called the Lamb more than anything else

in the Book of Revelation may be the most important truth that will unlock your understanding of the end times.

As you might expect, we must answer that question by applying the lens of the Old Testament. Simply put, Jesus is called the Lamb of God more than anything else in the last days because He is intricately connected to the Passover lamb used in the children of Israel's great deliverance and exodus out of Egypt. If we want to understand the Book of Revelation and the end times correctly, we must view them through the lens of the Passover experience.

Yeshua's mission on earth was to bring to fullness that which was revealed in primitive form through the ancient Israelites more than thirty-five hundred years ago. How were the Israelites saved? By the blood of the Passover lamb.

Let's turn to a pivotal passage of Scripture to learn more about this. In Exodus 12 God gave the Israelites instructions while they were still in Egypt:

> Every man shall take a lamb, according to the house of their fathers, a lamb for a household....Your lamb shall be without blemish, a male of the first year. You shall take it out from the sheep, or from the goats.... and then the whole assembly of the congregation of Israel shall kill it in the evening. They shall take some of the blood and put it on the two side posts and on the upper doorpost of the houses in which they shall eat it. They shall eat the flesh on that night, roasted with fire, and they shall eat it with unleavened bread and bitter herbs....In this way shall you eat it: with your waist girded, your sandals on your

feet, and your staff in your hand. So you shall eat it
in haste. It is the Lord's Passover.

For I will pass through the land of Egypt this
night and will smite all the firstborn in the land of
Egypt, both man and beast, and against all the gods
of Egypt I will execute judgment. I am the Lord. The
blood shall be to you for a sign on the houses where
you are. And when I see the blood, I will pass over
you, and the plague shall not be upon you to destroy
you when I smite the land of Egypt....Then Moses
called for all the elders of Israel and said to them,
"Draw out and take for yourselves a lamb according
to your families and kill the Passover lamb....And
when your children shall say to you, 'What does this
service mean to you?' that you shall say, 'It is the
sacrifice of the Lord's Passover, who passed over the
houses of the children of Israel in Egypt, when He
smote the Egyptians, and delivered our households.'"
—Exodus 12:3, 5–8, 11–13, 21, 26–27

That night the Lord did just as He said, passing through
Egypt and killing every firstborn in the land whose house was
not marked. It was a horrendous night, filled with anguish
and death. And yet for those whose doorposts were covered
by the blood of a perfect, spotless lamb, the Lord fulfilled
His promise to "pass over" them and keep them safe. It was
only after this night that the Israelites were released from
their bondage and led out of Egypt.

## REVELATION THROUGH THE PASSOVER LENS

The underlying theme of the Passover experience is God delivering His children out of Egypt through the blood of the lamb. This is the gospel in a nutshell: God has sent His Son, the perfect Lamb, to the earth to deliver us from the evil that rules this world. Just as God delivered the nation of Israel out of Egypt in ancient times, He will once again in the end times deliver His people from the "Egypt" that is this fallen world and the cosmic forces of darkness that permeate it.

This is a remarkable revelation for many people. It may even be the first time you have made the connection between what happened in Exodus and what happens in the Book of Revelation. Yet the further parallels between Israel's exodus and the world's salvation—both today and in the end times— are equally astounding. So let's take a look at some of the main "players" in each setting.

Egypt, as in the time of Israel's exodus, was a prophetic picture of the present world in which we live. For more than four hundred years the Israelites were in bondage. They were slaves to a wicked culture bent on keeping them in chains.

Pharaoh, the supreme ruler of Egypt, was a prophetic picture of Satan, whom the B'rit Hadashah (and even Yeshua) refers to as "the god of this world" (2 Cor. 4:4) or "the ruler of this world" (John 12:31). Pharaoh believed he was God, and the people indeed considered him a deity. His rule dominated every aspect of Egyptian culture, just as Satan's authority permeates every aspect of our world today.

We live in a world controlled by the "god of this world." Our world, along with all its principalities and powers, seeks to put people in slavery every day. And the ruler of this world wants nothing more than to keep those people bound. As a result, countless individuals are in bondage to such things as drugs, alcohol, money, pornography, time, their careers, sports—the list goes on and on. Many people on earth feel oppressed and beaten down in the same way the Israelites were in bondage to the Egyptians.

To that degree Israel was a prophetic picture of all God's people today. This does not mean that those who come to faith in the Messiah must literally become Jewish or become part of the nation of Israel. But in a prophetic sense all of God's children today—those who have been born again into Yeshua the Messiah, whether Jew or Gentile—are the "Israel of God" (Gal. 6:16).

The Passover lamb—the spotless lamb each Hebrew family sacrificed that night in Egypt—was, of course, Jesus. Even outside of the Book of Revelation this connection is made. John 1:29 says that when John the Baptist "saw Jesus coming toward him [he] said, 'Look, the Lamb of God, who takes away the sin of the world.'" And in 1 Corinthians 5:7 Paul wrote, "For Christ, our Passover lamb, has been sacrificed" (NIV).

What is interesting is that every Jewish family in Egypt was commanded to take and kill a lamb, according to Exodus 12. This was not just a ceremony conducted by priests, elected officials, or professionals for hire. Each family brought the lamb into its home for a season. The family members were to take it in, care for it, and love it as if it were one of them. Then, on the appropriate day of the month, they would take the lamb outside and put it to death. It was not just the father who quietly took the lamb behind the house and killed it without anyone seeing it. Instead every Israelite was commanded to take part in putting the lamb to death (Exod. 12:6).

Why do you think God instructed the Israelites to do it this way? Wasn't that a little too violent for the children? Didn't God understand family values?

God did this so that people in every generation after Yeshua's would recognize that we were all participants in His death. It was not just the Romans who killed Jesus, nor was it only the Jews; it was *every single one of us*. We all crucified the Lamb of God on the cross by the sin nature within each of us, regardless of our age or race or heritage. It was your sin and my sin that put Him on the cross two thousand years ago.

Despite our shared guilt in Jesus' death, we can each receive the blessing of His selfless sacrifice, just as every Israelite who killed the Passover lamb was blessed. Once the family took the blood of the lamb and put it over the doorpost of its home, the family was safe from harm. When the Lord passed through Egypt that night and saw the blood of a spotless lamb on the doorpost, He passed over that household. It did not matter if you were a good Hebrew or a bad one, whether you had prayed enough or sacrificed enough or tithed enough or anything else. The Lord was not looking for the righteousness of the individual. The only thing that mattered was whether you were covered by the lamb's blood.

It is no different for us today. Our works or attempts at righteousness, as good as they might be, do not earn us salvation. The only thing that saves us is being marked by the blood of the Lamb of God, Yeshua HaMashiach. First Peter 1:19 says we were redeemed "with the precious blood of Christ, as of a lamb without blemish and without spot." It is

*His* blood covering our lives that makes us righteous, holy, and cleansed when the great Judge sees us today. And just as powerfully it will be the same blood of the Lamb that will cover believers in the end times. His blood will mark them in such a way that they will be covered and protected from God's judgments and wrath. Revelation 9:4 describes a protection from judgment for those with "the seal of God on their foreheads." End-time believers will have a seal of protection because of the Lamb's blood covering them, just as ancient Israel was protected when the plagues fell.

Saying such a thing, however, predicates that believers—the church of Jesus Christ—will actually be here during the tribulation. And this, naturally, leads us into a discussion about the rapture, which is easily one of the most hotly debated topics concerning the end times.

## To Be (Here) or Not to Be (Here)

The rapture is the glorious event in which God will remove the church from the world. We will meet Jesus in the air and be transported into heaven. Although the word *rapture* is never used in Scripture, its meaning comes from two verses in 1 Thessalonians, in which Paul says:

> For the Lord Himself will descend from heaven with a shout, with the voice of the archangel, and with the trumpet call of God. And the dead in Christ will rise first. Then we who are alive and remain shall be *caught up together with them in the clouds to meet the Lord in the air.* And so we shall be forever with the Lord.
>
> —1 Thessalonians 4:16–17, emphasis added

For years believers have debated exactly when the rapture will take place. Rather than diving into specific verses to prove or disprove whether the church will be in the world or raptured out of it during the tribulation, for now it is important that we continue looking at the Book of Revelation through the lens of the Tanakh. Remember, the Bible is one complete story, which means there is a profound connection between its beginning parts (the events of the Torah) and its end parts (the events of Revelation).

Consider this: The ancient exodus of Israel out of Egypt is a prototype of the church being raptured out of the world when the "plagues" described in Revelation fall. When God judged Egypt in the Book of Exodus, he sent ten plagues. It is not coincidence that many of these plagues are virtually identical to the judgments that will be released upon earth during the great tribulation.

For example, the very first plague in Egypt was turning its waters into blood (Exod. 7:19). We find the exact same thing in Revelation 16:3–7 as the second and third bowls of God's wrath are poured out. God sent a plague of frogs upon Egypt in Exodus 8:1–2, and Scripture uses the same words to describe what is released during the sixth bowl of God's wrath (Rev. 16:13–14). Exodus 9:8–9 recounts the plague of boils sent upon the Egyptians, just as the first bowl releases this same thing on the Antichrist's followers (Rev. 16:2). The seventh plague upon Egypt, hail (Exod. 9:23–25), is replicated in both Revelation 8:7 and 16:21. Locusts are released in both Exodus 10:12–13 and Revelation 9:3–4 (albeit the latter kind sound *far* more terrifying!). God made the land dark just prior to Egypt's final plague, and He will bring about darkness at different times during the tribulation (Exod. 10:22–23; Rev. 6:12; 8:12–13; 16:10–11). And on and on it goes.

Do you see how intricately connected these two events are? We cannot view the judgments and wrath of the tribulation without taking into consideration what happened during the Exodus account. The two are intricately connected, as one is the shadow of the other. The plagues poured out locally on Egypt more than thirty-five hundred years ago are almost identical to the plagues that will be poured out upon the world during the tribulation. It is not by chance that there are not only similarities but also identical elements in comparing the Exodus account to the Revelation account. God is trying to tell us something!

What does all this—the ten plagues, the twenty-one end-time judgments, the similarities between the exodus and tribulation—have to do with the rapture? Everything! Let me explain.

Where were God's people, the children of Israel, during the ten plagues in the Book of Exodus? They were in Egypt. The Lord did not remove them before He began sending judgments upon Egypt; He kept His people there throughout. Yet He also kept them safe, protected, and unharmed during each of the plagues. That is not to say the Israelites did not feel the effects of God's judgments upon Egypt. They lived in the same land, so they most certainly felt the effects of an economy damaged by livestock shortage or freshwater rationing or ruined crops. And yet God always provided for and protected the million-plus Israelites living shoulder to shoulder with their Egyptian neighbors.

Based on everything I read in Scripture—the patterns of God throughout the *whole* Bible—I find it very difficult to believe that God will not do the same thing with His people during the end times. I believe that Israel's deliverance out of Egypt by the Passover lamb is a shadow for understanding how end-times events will play out. The fact that Yeshua is referred to as the Lamb twenty-nine times in the Book of Revelation bears witness to this.

As Israel was in Egypt when the plagues fell, I believe God's people will be on earth during most of the tribulation, but that He will supernaturally protect and provide for those who refuse to pledge allegiance to the Antichrist by taking the mark of the beast or by worshipping his image. Like the Israelites in Egypt, they will feel the effects of the end-time plagues; life will not be a walk in the park while those around them suffer. On the contrary, believers will have to rely upon the Lord's supernatural provision and protection on a daily basis. But the Lord is faithful, and He will provide, just as He did for the children of Israel.

## TIME TO GO

To find out when God will remove His people from the earth—when the rapture will take place—I believe we must apply the same principle we have throughout this chapter: We must view the Book of Revelation once again through the lens of the Tanakh and more specifically the Exodus account.

So when did God take the children of Israel out of Egypt? He kept them in the land throughout the ten plagues, even during the judgment of the firstborns that fell on Passover. But we must remember, that Passover night was not when God's final wrath was poured out upon Egypt. No, as bad as that was for the Egyptians, when all of their firstborn died, there was still something worse: the Red Sea.

The Egyptians—or more specifically, Pharaoh and thousands of his men—met their fate when God drowned them in the Red Sea. God removed His people from the land only when His final wrath was being poured out upon the Egyptians.

If we apply this principle to the Book of Revelation, we find that the full wrath of God does not begin until the seventh trumpet, which ushers in what John calls "the bowls of the wrath of God on the earth" (Rev. 16:1). In fact, many Bible scholars separate those in this last group by calling them outpourings of God's wrath, whereas the first fourteen are considered God's judgments. All are terrible in their own right. But it is obvious that the last seven are the worst, and they begin with the sounding of the seventh and last trumpet. Paul seemed to indicate that the church will be ushered out of the world right before them when he wrote, "In a moment, in the twinkling of an eye, at the last trumpet, for the trumpet will sound, the dead will be raised incorruptible, and we shall be changed" (1 Cor. 15:52). And as we already read in 1 Thessalonians:

> For the Lord Himself will descend from heaven with a shout, with the voice of the archangel, *and with the trumpet call of God.* And the dead in Christ will rise first. Then we who are alive and remain shall be caught up together with them in the clouds to meet the Lord in the air. And so we shall be forever with the Lord.
>
> —1 Thessalonians 4:16–17, emphasis added

Applying the Exodus lens, then, we can conclude that God will remove His people right before His worst judgment, or in this case, judgments. Just as God supernaturally parted the Red Sea and allowed Moses and all of Israel to pass through the waters to the other side, so He will part the "waters" of the heavens upon the seventh trumpet and translate His people to the other side of this world, which is with Him in heaven.

When all the Israelites had passed through to the other side, God closed the waters again and destroyed the Egyptian army in His wrath. I believe it will be the same way during the tribulation: When the church has been raptured, the Lord will close the curtains of heaven and pour out His full wrath upon those who remain on earth. He will cleanse the planet of its evil much like the waters came and washed away the wickedness of Egypt.

## A REMINDER FOR READINESS

Though it is obvious by now what I believe about the timing of the rapture, my point is less about when it will occur and more—far more—about the lens with which we understand the Book of Revelation as a whole. I hope I have challenged you enough to look into the Scriptures on your own and prayerfully ask the Holy Spirit to lead you into truth regarding God's judgments, His wrath, and the rapture.

Many people have grown up assuming the church will be raptured before any of "that fire and brimstone stuff" begins. They naively think God will come floating down during the good times and whisk away His people so we never have to face any problems. (And why not believe this when it would be so much easier and convenient?) When they hear someone talking about the tribulation or God's judgments, they quickly tune out and think, "Thank goodness I don't have to pay attention to all that scary stuff since I won't be here anyway."

Beloved, I do not believe this is biblical. Unfortunately, this "I won't have to deal with any of it" mentality has caused countless believers to never study the Word, much less the Book of Revelation. Worse still, it has caused them to be unprepared. Anyone can see that difficult times have already come. The economy is not getting better. Nations will not stop making nuclear weapons. Morality will continue to deteriorate. Chaos will increase throughout the earth. We are entering the last days.

The point of us talking about and studying the end times— ultimately, the point of this book—is not to gain more head knowledge so we can make better arguments to defend our position on when the rapture will occur. No, the point is that we need to be prepared for what lies ahead! Regardless of when you think the Lord will return, He wants you ready!

Let me put it another way. Do you think when Yeshua returns, the first question He will ask you is whether your theological stance on the rapture was correct? At that point it will matter about as much as finding a winning lottery ticket from 1902. The Book of Revelation is a guide for the bride of Christ so she will be ready when He comes. That is its main purpose. Yes, we can be more prepared when we understand what we're reading. And yes, to understand correctly requires reading it with the right lens. But even so, the point is not our reading; it's what we do in response to what we have read. Let's not forget this as we receive greater revelation about the times in which He will return so that we can be better prepared.

# CHAPTER 6

# ARMAGEDDON AND THE MESSIAH'S RETURN

EVERY GOOD STORY has a climax. Every *great* story has a climax that is unforgettable. In the award-winning movie *Gladiator*, for example, Roman general-turned-slave Maximus (played by Russell Crowe) literally fights his way through the gladiatorial ranks until a final showdown with the treacherous Emperor Commodus at last gives him the chance to avenge the murders of his wife and children. Or in the climactic scene of J. R. R. Tolkien's *The Lord of the Rings*, the main character, Frodo, stands above Mount Doom's volcanic fires with the chance once and for all to destroy the ring that has brought Middle Earth to the brink of destruction, and he wrestles to the end with the ring's otherworldly power to preserve itself.

These are great stories, each with a complicated plot that builds and builds to the point that we are on the edge of our seats in expectation of what will happen. But as intriguing as these and other fictional works are, they pale in comparison with the reality of what will be the climax of world history, as revealed in the Book of Revelation.

At the end of the tribulation most people left on earth will still be loyal to the Antichrist, even after God's judgments and wrath have wiped out the majority of life on the planet. These people's hearts will remain hardened to the Lord, filled with the same vitriol Satan has toward Him. Because of this blind allegiance to the Antichrist, something peculiar will happen between the sixth and seventh bowls of wrath. According to John's account in Revelation:

> Then I saw three unclean spirits like frogs coming out of the mouth of the dragon, out of the mouth of the beast, and out of the mouth of the false prophet. For they are spirits of demons, performing signs, who go out to the kings of the earth and of the whole world, to gather them to the battle of that great day of God Almighty....They gathered them together to the place which in Hebrew is called Armageddon.
> —REVELATION 16:13–14, 16

Under the leadership of the satanic "trinity" (Satan, the Antichrist, and the false prophet), the nations will be demonically summoned and empowered to gather for a final showdown against their shared enemy. This culminating battle is called Armageddon (*Har Magedon* or *Har Megiddo* in Hebrew), named for the valley in Israel where Revelation 16:16 says the enemy forces will gather.

Whether the final battle will actually take place exclusively in Har Magedon is unclear because Scripture mentions other Israeli locations as part of the conflict as well. Indeed the Hebrew prophets spoke about this climactic event in several passages of the Tanakh. For example, in Joel 3 we find the Lord describing the battle scene:

> I will gather all the nations, and bring them down to the Valley of Jehoshaphat. I will enter into judgment with them there regarding My people and My heritage Israel, whom they have scattered among the nations; they have also divided up My land....

Proclaim this among the nations: Consecrate a war!
Stir up the mighty men! Let all the men of war draw
near and rise. Beat your plowshares into swords and
your pruning hooks into spears; let the weakling
say, "I am a warrior!" Hurry and come, all you surrounding nations, and gather there. Bring down Your
warriors, O LORD. Let the nations be roused, and go
up to the Valley of Jehoshaphat; for there I will sit
to judge all the surrounding nations....Multitudes,
multitudes, in the valley of decision! For the day of
the LORD is near in the valley of the decision.
—JOEL 3:2, 9–12, 14

The Valley of Jehoshaphat literally means the "valley
where Yahweh judges," or as verse 14 says, the "valley of the
decision."[1]

We see from this passage that this is where God will judge
the nations. But it is important for us to understand that *God*
will establish this battle, not Satan or people. Although the
Antichrist and the nations of the world will assemble in a futile
attempt to defeat Jesus, it is God who, in His sovereignty, will
initiate this massive gathering. He wants to bring this conflict
to pass because in the end He will step in and destroy the enemy's attempts to corrupt this world beyond repair.

Before the Lord judges the nations, however, the global
landscape will be more intense than ever before. Joel says
the nations will be "roused" (v. 12). Think about it: As massive as the previous two world wars were, not every country
took part in them. So this end-time scene will be truly
remarkable in that it will include the whole world. Nations

will gather out of a common hatred for two main things: the Lord and His people, Israel.

## In Israel's Defense

In chapter 3 we saw how Satan's strategy to hurt God is to go after His children, as revealed in Revelation 12. Because the enemy knows He cannot touch Yeshua, He will "[persecute] the woman [Israel] who gave birth to the male Child [Jesus]" and "wage war with the remnant of her offspring" (Rev. 12:13, 17). Most Bible scholars interpret "the remnant of her offspring" to mean the church, and if that is correct, then at this point in the tribulation timeline believers will have already been raptured. That means only Israel will be left on the earth.

As has been the case so often in history, the Jewish people will feel alone, helpless, and as if they were looking down the barrel of every weapon on earth. Indeed the unified armies will cross Israeli borders thinking they once again have the Jewish people on the brink of extermination. Obviously hatred for the Jewish people will have emerged long before this time. Even today anti-Semitism is on the rise again. Yet there will be a point in time when this hatred for God's chosen people will climax and cause the nations to assemble at Har Magedon in an attempt to wipe out the seemingly defenseless, tiny nation of Israel.

If this sounds like a familiar story for Israel, that's because it is. Throughout Jewish history we find cases where the Jews were outnumbered, overpowered, and facing sure defeat. Yet repeatedly God rose to defend His people and vanquish their enemies.

So it will be in the end times. Israel's only hope will be

God, and yet He is always enough. God Himself will be their defense. Joel reminds us of this in His continuing depiction of Armageddon:

> The LORD roars from Zion, and sounds His voice from Jerusalem, and heaven and earth quake. But the LORD is a refuge for His people, and a stronghold for the children of Israel. Then you will know that I am the LORD your God, who dwells in Zion, My holy mountain. And Jerusalem will be holy, and invaders will never again pass through her.
>
> —JOEL 3:16–17

Once God defends Israel during this end-time offensive, He promises that "invaders will never again pass through her" (v. 17). This will be a miracle in itself, for Jewish history is filled with a long list of empires and nations conquering the children of Israel and ruling over their land.

It is important to note, however, that Joel 3 specifically mentions Jerusalem. While we are uncertain about other Israeli locations involved in Armageddon, there is no doubt Jerusalem will be the centerpiece of this culminating end-times battle. This is why many of the Hebrew prophets' descriptions of Armageddon specifically depict the assault on Jerusalem. Zechariah, for example, relayed the Lord's prophetic warning to those attacking Jerusalem:

> I am going to make Jerusalem a cup that sends all the surrounding peoples reeling. Judah will be besieged as well as Jerusalem. On that day, when all the nations of the earth are gathered against her, I will make Jerusalem an immovable rock for

all the nations. All who try to move it will injure themselves.

—ZECHARIAH 12:2–3, NIV

A few verses later the prophet reminded readers:

On that day the LORD will shield those who live in Jerusalem, so that the feeblest among them will be like David, and the house of David will be like God, like the angel of the LORD going before them. On that day I will set out to destroy all the nations that attack Jerusalem.

—ZECHARIAH 12:8–9, NIV

The Lord's promises will be a welcomed reminder for those in Jerusalem in the last days. Only two chapters later Zechariah offered a glimpse of the disturbing days in store for the city:

For I will gather all the nations against Jerusalem for battle. The city will be captured and the houses plundered and the women ravished. Half of the city will go to exile, but the remainder of the people will not be cut off from the city.

—ZECHARIAH 14:2

For a time it will appear that Jerusalem and all of Israel will be wiped off the map. Foreign armies will overtake the land, plunder its houses, rape the women, and take half the population as prisoners. It will be a horrific time, as if the Holocaust were beginning all over again. And by virtually all accounts it will be the end of Israel.

Yet just when it seems as if there is no hope for God's

chosen people, the Messiah will appear. Not only will He come to defend the Jewish people, but He will supernaturally make a way for their escape, offer them protection, and go to war on their behalf.

> Then the LORD will go forth and fight against those nations, as when He fights on a day of battle. In that day His feet will stand on the Mount of Olives, which is in front of Jerusalem on the east....Then the LORD, my God, will come, and all the holy ones with Him!
> —ZECHARIAH 14:3–5, NASB

Where does Zechariah say the Lord will come to save Israel? In one of the most amazing proofs of the unity of God's Word (the Bible), Yeshua will return to save Israel *in the exact spot where He last left earth!* In Acts 1 the Lord ascended to heaven, and Scripture records that the disciples "returned to Jerusalem from the Mount of Olives" (Acts 1:12). That means they watched Him ascend from the Mount of Olives. Where did Zechariah say Jesus will stand on the day of Armageddon? The Mount of Olives! His feet will hit the earth in the same place from which He ascended.

Don't you just love how precise God is with His plans? And isn't it wonderful how He has perfectly stitched together the Hebrew Bible (Old Testament) and the B'rit Hadashah (New Testament)? There is such power in understanding the unity of His Word!

Zechariah's account of Armageddon did not end there, however. He continued with a description that once again lines up perfectly with what the New Testament shares: "And on that day there will be no light. The lights will diminish. And there will be one day known to the LORD, neither during the day nor the night, but at the evening time there will be light" (Zech. 14:6–7).

As we examined in the last chapter, the Book of Revelation gives several accounts of the sun, moon, and stars darkening during the time of God's judgments. Yet the day of Armageddon will be unique given the cosmic activity surrounding it. Zechariah called it a day with "no light" (Zech. 14:6). The prophet Joel described it as a day in which "the sun and moon darken, and the stars withdraw their radiance" (Joel 2:10). And in Matthew 24:29 Jesus validated both Zechariah's and Joel's descriptions, saying, "Immediately after the tribulation of those days, 'the sun will be darkened, the moon will not give its light; the stars will fall from heaven, and the powers of the heavens will be shaken.'" Once again the Lord was attesting to the unity between the Hebrew Bible and New Testament.

Although the day of Armageddon will be marked by a great darkness, God's supernatural light will break into it. Zechariah said, "At the evening time there will be light" (Zech. 14:7), indicating that either the Lord will literally switch the earth's rotation or He will be the very light appearing in the evening—or both!

## COMING WITH THE CLOUDS

We find even more unity between the Tanakh and the New Testament in their description of what Jesus' return will look like. Six hundred years before Yeshua was born, the prophet Daniel had a vision of the Lord's second coming in a dream: "I saw in the night visions, and there was one like a Son of Man coming with the clouds of heaven" (Dan. 7:13).

Daniel was far from alone in his picture of Jesus coming with, in, or on the clouds of heaven. Indeed this is the same image associated with the Lord's appearing that is seen throughout the Bible. For example, when God revealed Himself to the children of Israel at Mount Sinai, He appeared in "a thick cloud on the mountain," accompanied by thunder, lightning, and a blaring trumpet (Exod. 19:16; see also verses 9, 19).

Though that may sound like a dramatic entrance, this is no fairy tale or make-believe story; Moses' description is a true historical account. How do we know this? Because you cannot explain the existence of the Jewish people today aside from the experience of God revealing Himself in a cloud at Mount Sinai! This event marked the Jewish people and set them apart from all nations. On that mountainside God's presence came to a relatively tiny group of people who have since survived countless attacks, massacres, and exiles through the ages. Yet the miracle of their survival can all be traced to this event. The fact that the Jewish people are alive today can be explained only by the truth that God really came to them in the clouds, as described in Exodus.

In Ezekiel 10:3–4 the Lord once again entered the scene—this time His temple—with a cloud of glory. Likewise in 2 Chronicles 5:13–14 the cloud of God's glory was so thick that "the priests were not able to stand in order to serve." These are historical accounts—records of Israel's actual history as a nation—not just fancy poetic writings. Throughout the rest of the Tanakh the Hebrew prophets describe the Lord's arrival in tandem with clouds, just as will be the case at Armageddon. (See 2 Samuel 22:10–12; Job 22:14; Psalm 97:2; Nahum 1:3.)

If we compare these examples in the Tanakh with several New Testament accounts, we will once again find amazing cohesion. In Matthew 26:64 Jesus told the Sanhedrin, "You will see the Son of Man seated at the right hand of Power and *coming on the clouds of heaven*" (emphasis added). Paul encouraged the believers in Thessalonica with a brief description of the Messiah's return, saying:

> For the Lord Himself will descend from heaven with a shout, with the voice of the archangel, and with the trumpet call of God....Then we who are alive and remain shall be caught up together with them *in the clouds* to meet the Lord in the air.
> —1 THESSALONIANS 4:16–17, EMPHASIS ADDED

Just as Acts 1:9 records that Yeshua ascended to heaven in a cloud, so shall He return to the earth in a heavenly cloud. John affirmed this in the Book of Revelation when he wrote: "Look! He is coming with clouds, and every eye will see Him, even those who pierced Him. And all the tribes of the earth will mourn because of Him" (Rev. 1:7).

Wait, what did John say? All the tribes of the earth will *mourn* because of Him? Why? This is the Messiah's long-awaited return, the day He *finally* comes back to the earth after countless generations and years of anticipation. This is when the King of kings and Savior of the world arrives, just as He promised! So why will everyone on earth mourn His return? Lest we forget, Jesus will not be a welcomed sight—or Savior—to all on that day.

## A DAY OF REJOICING OR RECKONING

Despite the diluted pop-culture references, Armageddon will mark a day of complete horror for most of those still on earth at that time. As believers we long for this day. It is when our beloved Savior returns to claim His rightful place on earth. We know He will remove everything in His way and establish His kingdom "on earth, as it is in heaven" (Matt. 6:10). Jesus will rule the earth, and we, as His beloved bride, will be established to reign with Him. Wow!

So for those who have put their trust in Jesus, His return will be a time of rejoicing. As Isaiah prophesied, "Then you shall see this, and your heart shall rejoice, and your bones shall flourish like an herb" (Isa. 66:14).

Yet for those unwilling to declare Jesus as their Lord, this will be the worst day in history—one that will actually never end for them. The Messiah's appearance will be cause for terror, as it will usher in a day of reckoning that will haunt them for all eternity. Yeshua's return will mark the point of no return for the vast majority of those still on earth. They will refuse to acknowledge Yeshua as Lord and Savior, despite having opportunity after opportunity to repent and receive God's mercy. Sadly, their stubbornness and hard-heartedness will be their demise.

Zechariah's depiction of what happens to these people during Armageddon makes today's horror movies seem tame.

> And this will be the pestilence with which the LORD will strike all the peoples who go to battle against Jerusalem: Their flesh will rot as they stand on their feet, their eyes will rot in their sockets, and their tongues will rot in their mouths.
> —ZECHARIAH 14:12

The Lord will strike those who rage against Him. Based on Zechariah's description, I imagine this to resemble the atomic bomb's effect on those upon whom it was released, as it literally burned the flesh off their bodies. Destruction will be everywhere they turn. In addition, Jesus will surround Himself with a whirlwind of fire and a host of heavenly armies that seems to include the raptured saints. (See Zechariah 14:5; Revelation 19:14.) When He comes, all rebellion will be silenced.

> For the LORD shall come with fire and with His chariots like a whirlwind, to render His anger with fury and His rebuke with flames of fire. For by fire and by His sword on all flesh, the LORD shall execute judgment; and the slain of the LORD shall be many.
>
> —ISAIAH 66:15–16

Isaiah's account matches up with John's depiction of the same scene in the Book of Revelation:

> I saw heaven opened. And there was a white horse. He who sat on it is called Faithful and True, and in righteousness He judges and wages war. His eyes are like a flame of fire, and on His head are many crowns....Out of His mouth proceeds a sharp sword, with which He may strike the nations. "He shall rule them with an iron scepter." He treads the winepress of the fury and wrath of God the Almighty. On His robe and on His thigh He has a name written: KING OF KINGS AND LORD OF LORDS. And I saw an angel standing in the sun, and he cried with a loud voice to all the birds flying in the midst of heaven, "Come and gather for the supper of the great God, to eat the flesh of kings, the flesh of commanders, the flesh of strong men, the flesh of horses and their

riders, and the flesh of all men, both free and slave, both small and great!" ...The remnant were slain with the sword which proceeded out of the mouth of Him who sat on the horse. And all the birds gorged themselves with their flesh.

—REVELATION 19:11–12, 15–18, 21

Many believe the sword in the Lord's mouth here is the power of His Word, and that by the authority of the Word He will slay those who oppose Him. Whether the sword is literal or figurative, the end result is the same: His enemies will be utterly destroyed. And just as Zechariah did, John depicts the true horror of this day by describing how birds will "gorge" themselves on the millions of dead bodies strewn throughout Israel.

This is not some fictional horror story, however. The Tanakh and B'rit Hadashah are graphic in their depiction of this end-times showdown for one main reason: to wake us up so that we will be prepared. How do I know this? Let's take a look at one of the most curious words Jesus spoke in the Book of Revelation.

## READY FOR HIS RETURN

We have read John's account of the global calamities unleashed upon earth from the heavens. Yet amid all the destruction, chaos, and catastrophe, the apostle suddenly inserted a word spoken directly from the Lord to His people, as if He were pulling us aside to share a secret. It begins with a completely unexpected phrase: "Look, I am coming as a thief" (Rev. 16:15).

Why would the Prince of Peace—the safest person in the

universe—compare His return to a thief breaking into your house? Simply put, because no one *expects* a thief to come. You can't predict when a thief will try to break into your home; you can only prepare for it. And this is exactly why Jesus continued His sudden warning with: "Blessed is he who watches and keeps his garments on, lest he walk naked and his shame be exposed" (Rev. 16:15).

We might think this is a strange warning delivered at an even stranger time. Indeed the Lord wedges this between two verses about the satanic trinity gathering and empowering the nations against Him. And yet there is actually nothing strange or unfamiliar about the message, given how often Jesus told His followers to be ready for His return.

Perhaps you have heard the comedienne who jokes about her mother routinely reminding her to wear clean underwear in case she ever gets in an accident and has to go to the hospital. This may seem silly, and yet Jesus' warning to keep your "garments on" to avoid getting caught "naked" upon His return is no laughing matter. No one but the Father knows the exact time of the Lord's return (Matt. 24:36); therefore His coming for many will seem as sudden and unexpected "as a thief" (Rev. 16:15). Getting caught off guard by a break-in at your house is not good, but getting caught off guard by the second coming will be a matter of eternal life or death. Now *that's* bad!

Yeshua blatantly emphasized this point in the parable of the ten virgins. In the story, recorded in Matthew 25:1–13, all ten virgins took lamps to go out and meet the bridegroom. They knew he would come; they just didn't know how late it might be. Five of the virgins were content to bring lamps without any extra oil because they assumed their potential husband-to-be would come soon enough.

Upon his return, when the call went out deep into the night that he had finally arrived, these five virgins were left unprepared for the darkness. The five prepared virgins had brought enough extra oil for themselves and were ready for his coming. But the five foolish virgins had to go buy oil. And while they were out trying to get prepared, the doors to the wedding banquet were shut.

The parable's end-times connection became even more obvious when Yeshua added this twist to the story: When the five foolish virgins asked for the doors to be open, they were not merely told that the hall was full or that they needed to come back later. No, instead the bridegroom said, "Truly I say to you, I do not know you" (Matt. 25:12). Ouch! In the last days many will call upon Jesus for mercy after rejecting Him for so long. They will act as if their last-ditch effort to save themselves will be enough to restore the relationship He always wanted. And yet in that moment He will say He never knew them.

This is why we must be ready. We must be alert to His thief-like coming. We must be prepared for His arrival, no matter how late.

The Lord wants to help us be prepared. He does not just leave us on our own with a detached farewell—"Good luck with all that; hope it goes well!" No, the very Bridegroom whose return we await is also willing to gently guide us through the preparation process, if we will allow Him. And as any bride knows, getting prepared for your wedding definitely takes some work!

## CLEANING AND CLEANSING

I have told this story before, but the encounter was so profound I wanted to share it again here, especially for those who have never heard it. A few years ago I dreamed that my wife and I were traveling and stopped to stay the night at the home of my former martial arts instructor. When we arrived, he took us upstairs to show us where we would be staying—and promptly guided us into the bathroom. (If you think that's weird, you haven't heard anything yet!) Suddenly he jumped into the toilet bowl and was shrunk down inside a translucent egg. I could see him inside the egg, surrounded by blue sanitizing fluid, and yet he was joyful, content, and safe. A few seconds later he was standing beside us again, back in full stature and acting as if everything was normal.

The dream continued with my wife and me making our bed the following morning and going downstairs to tell my former instructor that we were leaving. To our surprise he stopped us in our tracks. "Not so fast," he said. "Let's go up into the bedroom and make sure you're ready to leave."

I was taken aback, but we went upstairs, and he began inspecting the room. I knew we had made the bed and cleaned up. In addition, we had stayed for only one night; how much mess could we have made?

I was stunned, then, when my martial arts instructor pulled the dresser in the room away from the wall, took out a toothbrush, and began scrubbing the wall by the baseboard behind the dresser. "You've got to scrub behind here before you leave," he instructed.

He then reached behind the dresser, pulled out something that looked like an electrical box, and told me to set it up correctly. I had never seen anything like this. It was attached to the wall by what looked like telephone wire and appeared to have only a single button on top. So I "set it up" by doing the only thing I knew to do: I pushed the button.

"You're doing it wrong!" my teacher said. "You're not thinking. Here, let me show you." And with that he got down on his knees, grabbed the gadget, and flipped open a side panel on it (which I had not seen). Suddenly I could see that this gadget had many buttons inside. He entered a combination and reset the device, and then the dream ended.

I awoke with a strong sense that this dream, despite being strange, was directly from God. So I asked Him to reveal its meaning.

"You and your wife are on a journey," I sensed Him saying to me. "But before you can continue on this journey, we need to clean up the filth in your heart and in your life. I am sanitizing you from the scum you picked up living in this world, through your own sin, and through generational curses. I'm cleansing you of that filth so you are able to move on."

He then explained the second part of my dream, involving cleaning behind the dresser. "I want to scrub deeper than you realize," I felt Him saying. "You think things are all right as they are, that as long as things look good from the outside, everything is fine. And to your credit, you have tried to deal with many issues in your life. You have tried to clean as much as you could. But I want to go much deeper. I want to cleanse you from deep within your heart."

"But what about the electrical box thing? What was that?" I asked.

"I want to reset your thinking," He explained. "But to reset it I need you to begin thinking about what you are thinking. You assumed one thing about the box because that's all you could see, but you weren't *thinking* the way I want you to. I need to reset the way you process things so that you can capture every thought. I want to reprogram your mind so you can move forward in your journey. And you will experience great joy when you are sanctified, just as your martial arts instructor in your dream had great joy inside the sanitizing solution."

The Lord was tenderly preparing me through this experience. He continues to do so—to go deeper in cleansing my heart and teaching me how to capture every thought. He knows exactly what I need to do for the next step so I can continue my journey with Him. And He wants me to be ready to meet Him.

He wants the same for you. He wants to prepare you for His return so you will not have to worry about whether you will be accepted by Him at His coming. Instead you will be prepared for whenever He arrives.

Someday soon we will all meet God. We need to be like the five wise virgins—prepared and ready. That means we must cooperate with the Holy Spirit and His process of sanctifying us. He wants us to think more as He thinks, to act more as He acts, and to have more of His heart. To continue growing, we must be open to the Holy Spirit and yield to His work in our lives. The ultimate goal in studying these different aspects of the end times is not just to gain head knowledge. He wants to draw us to Him now so that we will not be caught off guard when He returns but instead will be taken into the wedding banquet and enjoy eternity with Him as His prepared bride.

# CHAPTER 7

# THE MARRIAGE BETWEEN GOD AND HIS PEOPLE

A T SOME POINT in life we all ask the same question: "Why am I here?"

The need to find purpose for our existence sets humans apart from the rest of creation, yet it is also what has frustrated humanity since the beginning of our history. The truth is, God created us for a deep purpose. As we all know, however, people search for that ultimate purpose in all the wrong places. Many people waste years of their lives following pop culture's advice to "look within yourself" for meaning. Their search for purpose revolves entirely around themselves as they ask only self-centered questions concerning their existence. But as created beings we must look to our Creator to understand what we are created for.

In this chapter we will discuss what I believe is the ultimate answer to the question of why we exist. This reason for our existence is also the driving force behind history's most exciting event. When Jesus returns to earth, not only will He wipe out His enemies at Armageddon and establish His millennial kingdom, but also something else will happen that the Book of Revelation calls the "marriage supper of the Lamb."

> Then I heard something like the sound like a great
> multitude, as the sound of many waters and as the
> sound of mighty thunderings, saying: "Alleluia! For
> the Lord God Omnipotent reigns! Let us be glad and

rejoice and give Him glory, *for the marriage of the Lamb has come*, and His wife has made herself ready. It was granted her to be arrayed in fine linen, clean and white." Fine linen is the righteous deeds of the saints. Then he said to me, "Write: Blessed are those who are invited to *the marriage supper of the Lamb*."
　　　　　　　—REVELATION 19:6–9, EMPHASIS ADDED

The "marriage supper of the Lamb" will be the greatest moment in history, the climax of humanity, and the destiny for which we were all made—all wrapped into one. It will be a cosmic event that surpasses our wildest imaginations and dwarfs every source of joy we currently have.

How do I know it will be so great? Because before it ever begins, John says we should "be glad and rejoice" when that day comes because "blessed are those who are invited" to this incredible event. Simply put, the marriage supper of the Lamb will be the culmination of everything Scripture points to regarding the relationship between God and His people.

## MARRIAGE MYSTERY

Did you know that Jesus is engaged and one day will be married? Jesus didn't just die on the cross to save you, but He purchased you with His own life to marry you. That may sound strange to you since we rarely hear preaching about this today. In fact, some people may find it odd that John mentioned such a marriage amid all the massive, often terrifying apocalyptic events described in Revelation. After all, only chapters before, John painted a picture of the world in complete chaos and destruction (Rev. 16), of the great harlot drunk from the blood of the saints (Rev. 17), and of Babylon burning in ruins (Rev. 18). That's not exactly the context in which you would expect to hear of a timeless romance, is it? Yet everything that happens during the end times—from the rise of history's most satanically empowered forces to God's cleansing of the earth with His judgments—essentially points to the union between Christ and His bride, the church.

Marriage is the ultimate union on earth. When a man and woman are married, they receive God's amazing gift of becoming one. This oneness is called *echad* in Hebrew and is first described in the Book of B'resheet (Genesis): "Therefore a man will leave his father and his mother and be joined to his wife, and they will become one flesh" (Gen. 2:24). An obvious aspect of being "one flesh" is the physical unity expressed through sex, which God intended to be a gift preserved for marriage. In fact, this sexual union is so powerful that one of its fruits—new life—mimics the very creative nature of God.

But as any husband or wife knows, the oneness of marriage is not just about sex and procreation. Marriage involves a coming together on every level—physical, spiritual, emotional, mental, and social. When Paul wrote about marriage in Ephesians 5, he explained that he was not merely talking about the union between a man and a woman but also about the end-times union of Christ and the church. He had seen a glimpse of this divine marriage, which is why he said, "This is a great mystery, but I am speaking about Christ and the church" (Eph. 5:32).

The great mystery Paul spoke of is the end-times union between Yeshua and His bride. This mystery is so profound that the earthly picture we have of marriage is but a mere shadow of what we will experience when we, the bride of Christ, are joined together with Jesus in the sky. When He returns, He will fully marry His people, merging with us to a degree we cannot imagine. God will so fill us with Himself and flow through us that we will be consumed with Him. And this will satisfy every longing in the human heart. Why? Because it is the ultimate reason for which we were made!

From the beginning we were created to be one with God Himself. Before the world was made, He who lacked nothing—who is perfectly complete in Himself—desired to have companionship with you and me. Think about that! We find this truth evident from the very first chapter of the first book of the Hebrew Bible.

> Then God said, "Let us make man in our image, after our likeness, and let them have dominion over the fish of the sea, and over the birds of the air, and over the livestock, and over all the earth, and over every creeping thing that creeps on the earth." So God created man in His own image; in the image of God He created him; male and female He created them.
>
> —GENESIS 1:26–27

As Creator the Lord has a relationship with all His creation. He has a relationship with everything mentioned in these verses—the fish, birds, livestock—and everything unmentioned. Even Jesus referred to this relationship with nature when He said that if people wouldn't praise Him, the rocks would (Luke 19:40). Notice, however, that none of these other creations, whether living or inanimate, were made in His image.

So why did the Lord create us uniquely in His image? For a unique relationship! He desired to have a special relationship with us, one that would be more intimate than His relationship with anything else in creation and surpass all others in its oneness with Him. Sounds a little bit like marriage, now doesn't it? That's because in mankind, God purposed a marriage relationship. Just as a husband desires to be one with his wife, God desires to be one with us and *has* ever since He first made us.

Our God is a God of relationship. In fact, you cannot find a biblical definition of who God is without including this aspect. It is one of the elements that sets Him apart from the gods of all the world's religions. Our God desires true, living relationship because He is a relational, living being. This is reflected in His very triune nature. Within the Trinity exists a supreme, perfect relationship among the Father, Son, and Holy Spirit. This is why in Genesis 1:1 God is called Elohim in Hebrew. The word Elohim, meaning God, is in plural form there. I am not saying that there is more than one God—there is only one God—but within God relationship exists. God is one, and yet He is multidimensional in His nature.

This concept of relationship existing within God is illustrated in the creation account, where we read of how God said, "Let *us* make man in *our* image, after *our* likeness" (Gen. 1:26, emphasis added). Who was He talking to there? Who is the "us," and who is the "our"? Some rabbis claim it was the angels, but the rest of Scripture proves the Lord was addressing the relationship existing within the triune Godhead. This is why John begins his Gospel by describing

Jesus as being "at the Father's side" (John 1:18). Many Bible versions translate this phrase to mean He is "in the bosom of the Father" (KJV, NASB, NKJV), while the New International Version says He is "in closest relationship with the Father." However it is described, this is the ultimate relationship through which all other relationships are based.

## MADE IN HIS IMAGE

Now that we have established that there is relationship within God via the Father, Son, and Holy Spirit, I would like to take this one step further and explore the maleness and femaleness of God. Although God is always addressed in the masculine, consider that He made mankind in His own image, both male and female (Gen. 1:27). God separated the feminine from the masculine when He took an element from the man to create the woman (Gen. 2:21–22). From this we can conclude that God has within Himself both the masculine and feminine.

Putting all this together—that within God is relationship, and within Himself exists both male and female—consider how this plays out in the relationship between a husband and wife. Their marriage to each other is meant to be a reflection of their oneness with God and a shadow of the relationship between Jesus, who is described in Scripture as the Bridegroom (Matt. 25), and the church, described as "the wife of the Lamb" (Rev. 21:9).

Humans were created as unique beings in God's image. The Lord's ultimate goal is to bring us back—to restore union—with Him. This is what the "marriage supper of the Lamb" is all about and why it will be the most wonderful event in human history. Just as a husband and wife become one flesh in every way, so we will become one with God in every way.

Jesus made a way for us to be one with the Father through His sacrifice on the cross. The power of the cross and Yeshua's victory over sin will never be lost, even a million years from now. But it is not until the marriage supper of the Lamb that we will be completely reunited with Him and experience total oneness with Him. Again, Jesus didn't die just to save us but also to marry us—and He has already purchased us with His blood.

In Jewish culture a bride would be betrothed to her fiancé and "bought" with a dowry that signified the binding nature of this contract. We have been betrothed to Yeshua, "bought" with the highest price—His very life—and are now in the process of being prepared for Him, as was Esther, who prepared and beautified herself before marrying the king (Est. 2:12–13). One day we will be officially wed to our Savior. The bride and Bridegroom will finally be one!

## A PROGRESSIVE REVELATION

Before we continue looking at this wonderful end-times event called the "marriage supper of the Lamb," it is important that we understand a theological concept called *progressive revelation*. Don't worry; even if you are just starting to study God's Word, the concept is simple enough. Progressive revelation is the idea that God reveals Himself increasingly over time rather than all at once. Because of this, the revelation of who God is becomes clearer as time passes.

For example, God revealed to us in the Old Testament that the means by which He can forgive sin is through the innocent dying in place of the guilty. We see this in the sacrificial system established in the early temple. It was not until after Jesus came to earth and died in the flesh, as revealed in the New Testament, that this concept was fully revealed and understood. This is just one aspect of how the revelation of God becomes clearer as time unfolds and crystallizes in the person of Jesus.

Paul described this idea of progressive revelation when he told the Roman believers he had preached the gospel "according to the revelation of the mystery, which was kept secret for long ages past, but now is revealed by the prophetic Scriptures according to the commandment of the everlasting God" (Rom. 16:25–26). What once was "kept secret" was suddenly being revealed to the Gentile believers of Rome.

Likewise the writer of Hebrews says, "God, who at various times and in diverse ways spoke long ago to the fathers through the prophets, has in these last days spoken to us by His Son, whom He has appointed heir of all things, and through whom He made the world" (Heb. 1:1–2). Both these scriptures show how during the period in which the Old Testament was being written, revelations of God were like shafts of light breaking into a dark room. Yet now the ceiling has been lifted off the room, and through Yeshua the whole sun is shining upon us. This is the New Testament era in which we live.

Keeping this idea of progressive revelation in mind, I want us now to look at how the concept of the marriage of the Lamb unfolds throughout the Tanakh (Old Testament) and becomes clearer in the B'rit Hadashah (New Testament).

## A MATTER OF DESIRE

Most marriages can be traced back to a single point in time when one partner desired the other. So it is in the relationship between God and His people. In the Tanakh, throughout the book of Sh'mot (Exodus), we find God making known His desire for the Jewish people. When the children of Israel were still slaves in Egypt, He told Pharaoh (through Moses) to release them so they might come to meet with Him in the wilderness (Exod. 5:1). After the Lord led His people out of Egypt, He reminded them at Mount Sinai, "You have seen what I did to the Egyptians, and how I lifted you up on eagles' wings, and brought you to Myself" (Exod. 19:4). His desire to be with His people prompted Him to come closer to them in a thick cloud upon Mount Sinai, yet they were so terrified they stayed at a distance and begged Moses to speak to the Lord on their behalf (Exod. 20:19–21).

Despite such rejection from the children of Israel, which sadly became a pattern, the Lord repeatedly expressed His heart to be close to them. In Exodus 25:8, He continued reaching out: "Let them make Me a sanctuary that I may dwell among them."

This was His desire all along: to dwell with His people. He did not deliver Israel out of Egypt just to free them from slavery. That was important, and He obviously wanted to see them released from bondage. But He also delivered them to bring them close to Him. He knew that in Him was the only place they would find true liberty. More so God simply longed to be with His people, just as a husband longs to be with his wife.

That has not changed. More than three thousand years later God still longs to be with His people. He wants to be with you. He wants to be with me. As amazing as that truth is—that the God of the universe truly desires to be with us—it can be too hard for some of us to accept.

As a result, many of us respond the same way the Israelites did at Sinai: We avoid God's invitation for intimacy and opt to stay at a distance from Him. Granted, we may say and do all the right things, obeying all the rules and being morally good. We may show up in church, tithe, and serve faithfully in ministry. But when it comes to being truly intimate with God, we cringe. We find it difficult to open our hearts. We would rather let that be something the worship team does. They're more prone to that kind of lovey-dovey stuff, right?

Beloved, the Bible is filled with God's warnings to those who think they can go through life doing all the "right" things but never loving Him the way He asks to be loved. In Isaiah 29:13 the Lord describes people who do this as ones who "draw near with their mouths and honor Me with their lips, but have removed their hearts far from Me." Sadly, when their time on earth is done and they face Him at the judgment seat, they will hear Him say the same haunting words spoken to the five foolish virgins locked out of the wedding feast: "I do not know you" (Matt. 25:12).

This is why Jesus, when asked what the greatest commandment was, did not hesitate to say, "You shall love the Lord your God with all your heart, and with all your soul, and with all your mind" (Matt. 22:37). God wants us to love Him with everything we have because that is exactly how He loves us! He is looking for a partner in love.

## A PROPHETIC PICTURE

This theme is repeated throughout the Scriptures, but we see it most profoundly in the Song of Songs. On its face, the Song is simply a love poem Solomon wrote to the woman he was about to marry, called the Shulamite bride. But my belief, and the belief of many others, is that the Holy Spirit gave the Song of Songs to the church to help us understand Jesus' love for us. It uses the marriage relationship as a paradigm for the relationship we have entered into with Him and reveals to us the heart and emotions of God more fully than any other book in the Bible.

I contend that the Song is a picture of Christ and the church. How can I say this with confidence? In 2 Peter 1:20–21, the apostle Peter writes:

> But know this first of all, that no prophecy of Scripture is a matter of one's own interpretation. For no prophecy at any time was produced by the will of man, but holy men moved by the Holy Spirit spoke from God.

Peter affirmed that all Scripture is written by the Holy Spirit. The primary role of the Holy Spirit is to glorify Messiah Jesus and disclose the deep things of Yeshua to us. So it is inconceivable that the Holy Spirit would have given us a book in the Bible that was only about King Solomon's natural relationship with his wife. Rather, everything in Scripture speaks of Jesus. Men were "moved by the Holy Spirit," and they spoke and wrote about God.

We also read in Luke 24 that *"beginning with Moses and with all the prophets,"* Jesus explained to His disciples *"the things concerning Himself in all the Scriptures"* (v. 27, NASB). This tells us plainly that not only is all Scripture written by the Holy Spirit, but all Scripture is about Jesus. The entire Word of God finds its ultimate purpose in Yeshua. He is the center focus of the whole Bible. So the Song of Songs must be about Messiah Jesus or it would not be in the Bible.

I do not believe Solomon knew when he wrote the Song of Songs that he was bringing forth a revelation beyond the natural one he had in mind. We find many instances in Scripture where people were moved by the Holy Spirit to speak and write in an inspired way—and didn't even know it. One example is in John 11, when Caiaphas told the chief priests and Pharisees, "It is expedient for you that one man die for the people, and that the whole nation not perish" (v. 50, NASB). The Bible says plainly that "he did not say this on his own initiative, but being high priest that year, he prophesied that Jesus was going to die for the nation" (John 11:51, NASB).

Just as Caiaphas prophesied without knowing it, I feel certain that when Solomon wrote the Song of Songs, he was not aware he was prophesying by the Holy Spirit. So what exactly was the Holy Spirit prophesying through Solomon?

In the context of the rest of Scripture, and in alignment with the prophetic nature of all the Scriptures, the Song of Songs speaks to the unparalleled depth of relationship we as believers have with our King, Jesus. We are His bride, journeying toward the marriage supper of the Lamb (Rev. 19:9). Marital intimacy is the only natural experience that approaches the close, loving relationship and partnership we were made to have with our Messiah.

As we saw previously, Paul unveiled a great mystery in Ephesians 5:32, which is that Christ and His church are exemplified in the earthly marriage relationship. Our marriages are little, lived-out pictures of the kind of relationship Jesus intends to have with us. So when the Shulamite bride boldly declares, "May he kiss me with the kisses of his mouth!" (Song 1:2, NASB), she is modeling the desire Jesus wants us to have for Him. And when the bridegroom responds to her longing with comments such as, "How beautiful you are, my darling, how beautiful you are!" (Song 4:1, NASB), and, "Your mouth like the best wine" (Song 7:9, NASB), his words reflect the way Messiah Jesus, our Bridegroom King, feels about us.

The reality is that Jesus gets great delight from our union with Him. He isn't marrying a bride from whom He receives no enjoyment. No, Yeshua enjoys His bride just as Solomon enjoyed the Shulamite. Messiah Jesus has emotions and is moved by our emotions. (See Luke 10:21, John 11:35, Matthew 14:14.) As in any close relationship, what we feel touches Him, and vice versa. The Song of Songs gives us the fullest revelation of the emotions of God, helping us to understand how Jesus feels about us and how we affect Him.

God has destined us to be married to Him. Every second of every day God is not just aware of us but keyed in on our emotions and thoughts. "The very hairs of your head are all numbered" (Luke 12:7, NASB). The journey into divine romance depicted in the Song of Songs is about our discovering that this relationship is real. We don't just get saved and go to heaven. We are the bride of Christ, His eternal partner, the joy of His heart.

Revelation 19:7–9 (NASB) says:

"Let us rejoice and be glad and give the glory to Him, for the marriage of the Lamb has come and His bride has made herself ready." It was given to her to clothe herself in fine linen, bright and clean; for the fine linen is the righteous acts of the saints. Then he said to me, "Write, 'Blessed are those who are invited to the marriage supper of the Lamb.'" And he said to me, "These are true words of God."

You and I have been called to experience such a deep relationship with Yeshua that we can only compare that type of love to the love between a husband and wife. The Holy Spirit used Solomon to give the church an understanding of how God feels about us and the type of love relationship we are being called into. As the events of Revelation unfold, you and I are heading into a relationship with Jesus so deep and so close that we have not even begun to perceive the fullness of it. We have been saved to be the bride of the Messiah, whose heart burns with a fiery love for us.

# CHAPTER 8

# A GRIEVING GOD

THE LORD LOOKS at us, His people, with more desire than even the most loving husband has for his wife. God is the very definition of love; therefore when He declares His love for us, we must realize that this perfect love for us is unending. We are the object of His complete affection. And this is also why the Lord grieves when His beloved continues to turn away from Him. Unfortunately the Tanakh includes a long history of the bride refusing the Bridegroom's love for her.

In Jeremiah 31:32, for example, the Lord promises to make a new marriage covenant with the children of Israel: "It will not be according to the covenant that I made with their fathers in the day that I took them by the hand to bring them out of the land of Egypt, because they broke My covenant, although I was a husband to them."

Israel's unfaithfulness is central to many prophetic books in the Old Testament. For example, the entire Book of Hosea deals with the picture of a husband pursuing his wife even when she is continually unfaithful. God told the prophet Hosea to marry a prostitute as a prophetic sign to Israel: "Then the LORD said to me, 'Go, again, love a woman who is loved by a lover and is committing adultery, just as the LORD loves the children of Israel, who look to other gods'" (Hos. 3:1). Hosea's wife would not stay committed and was intimate with others, and God's chosen people were the same way with Him.

Because of Israel's repeated unfaithfulness, God actually withdrew Himself. Anyone in relationship knows that the more intimate you become with someone, the more vulnerable you are. With vulnerability comes risk, and when you get hurt, the natural response is to withdraw. So is it any wonder that God withdrew when Israel abused His love so badly?

Now, God is invincible—that is the truth. He is all-powerful and in control of everything. But just as Jesus was crushed and wounded in the flesh, the Lord has made Himself so vulnerable in His love for us that we can actually hurt Him to the point that He grieves. Jesus wept, was touched by humanity, and was often moved with compassion for people. The Lord is so great, yet as the humblest person in the universe, He voluntarily chooses to allow Himself to be touched by human beings. Even as He wept at Lazarus' death, so too He is touched by us.

We can either bring Him joy or hurt Him. This is why the scripture says, "Do not grieve the Holy Spirit of God" (Eph. 4:30). To *grieve* means "to cause to suffer."[1] It involves hurt, distress, and even wounding. Yet this is what the Scripture says we can do to God's Spirit. It is a powerful revelation to understand how sensitive God is and to realize that you and I can actually hurt Him. By the same token, then, it gives Him immense pleasure when we voluntarily choose to love Him.

Can you imagine if you married a spouse who was robotic and only responded to you out of duty rather than from his or her heart? You would not find much joy or pleasure in your partner; in fact, that would be a miserable relationship!

We were made to be partners with the Lord in love. Yeshua is seeking a true bride. It's not just that He loves us;

He is looking for us to respond to His love and to love Him back. And this is why our relationship with Him is called a marriage.

First John 4:19 says, "We love Him because He first loved us." Sadly, our mistreatment of His love can cause Him to withdraw His presence, just as He did with the children of Israel. He does not ever *want* to withdraw His presence. Remember, He longs to be with us, His people. But He wants a people who love Him and welcome His presence rather than refuse Him at every opportunity. His desire, then, is that we begin to love Him the way He loves us—wholeheartedly, faithfully, and with complete devotion.

It is exciting to think that someday the body of Christ will reach this point. This is not some far-fetched fairy tale ending. When we, the church, meet Yeshua in the marriage of the Lamb, we will actually be a spotless bride, ready to be united with Him (Eph. 5:27). That means our love for Him will be pure. At the marriage supper of the Lamb all heaven will celebrate a bride who is ready to return the overwhelming love of the Bridegroom. We may never match His love—He is God, after all—but because we are made in His image, we can certainly love Him the way He desires.

## A LOVING GOD

Every bride remembers preparing herself on her wedding day: the hours of prepping her gown, veil, and train—steaming the dress to ensure every wrinkle is gone and every crease is in the right place. Then there are the hours of hairstyling, putting on makeup, getting dressed—it typically makes for a crazy day. And yet the moment a bride walks down the aisle to her husband-to-be, it is all worth it.

The day of our future marriage to Jesus will be like no other. The church h_s been preparing for that day for more than two thousand years, and we will continue to prepare until the moment our Husband appears. But what makes the marriage of the Lamb so different from all others is not only that it involves a divine marriage but also that the Lord Himself is the One readying us. This once again shows the level of His overwhelming love for us. In the Book of Ezekiel we find this truth prophetically portrayed:

> Now when I passed by you and looked upon you, you were old enough for love. So I spread My garment over you and covered your nakedness. Indeed, I swore to you, and entered into a covenant with you, says the Lord GOD, and you became Mine. Then I washed you with water. Indeed, I thoroughly washed away your blood from you, and I anointed you with oil. I clothed you also with embroidered work, and put sandals of porpoise skin on your feet, and girded you about with fine linen, and covered you with silk. I decked you also with ornaments, and put bracelets on your hands, and a chain on your neck. I put a jewel on your forehead, and earrings in your ears, and a beautiful crown on your head. Thus you were decked with gold and silver. And your raiment was of fine linen, and silk, and embroidered work. You ate fine flour, and honey, and oil. And you were exceedingly beautiful and advanced to royalty. Then your renown went out among the nations for your

beauty. For it was perfect through My comeliness
which I had put upon you, says the Lord GOD.
                                        —EZEKIEL 16:8–14

Incredibly, the Israelites rejected the Lord after receiving
this word from the prophet. They turned their backs on Him
and endured unnecessary pain as a result. It would be easy
to sit in judgment of them, but how often do believers today
do the same? How often do we reject the truth of who we
are in Yeshua and how much He loves us? How often do we
listen to the enemy's lies rather than believe Jesus loves and
accepts us individually, personally, and directly.

The reality is that the Lord has adorned us with beauty
and takes immense pleasure in us. In fact, Isaiah 62:5 says
that "as the bridegroom rejoices over the bride, so your God
shall rejoice over you." In Zephaniah 3:17 we hear more
about the extent of this rejoicing:

> He will rejoice over you with gladness, He will
> renew you with His love, He will rejoice over you
> with singing.

Those familiar with this verse know that the original
word for the second *rejoice, guwl* in Hebrew, means to spin
around wildly with excitement and joy.[2]

God twirls with absolute delight over us. That is the truth,
as declared in God's own Word! But let's be honest; how
many of us ever picture a Bridegroom God who loves us this
much? Most of the scriptures I have quoted in this chapter
are essentially God saying "I love you" to His people—and
that includes you. But sometimes we can become so accus-
tomed to hearing the phrase "God loves you" that the words

lose their meaning. Sometimes our hearts can become so hardened by life that we need more than words.

Maybe your perception of a husband's love has been so tainted, or even ruined, by the mistakes of your earthly husband or father that it is difficult to imagine a love this pure. Maybe the love I have been describing does not seem real. Or maybe you have started to believe the Lord's love is for everyone but you. You may carry such guilt or shame in your life that believing that God loves you is as overwhelming a challenge as scaling Mount Everest.

Let me emphasize that these are not my words. They are not some preacher's words or a pep talk from some motivational speaker. These are from God Himself: "I have loved you with an everlasting love; therefore with lovingkindness I have drawn you" (Jer. 31:3).

God's love for each of us is beyond what the world offers. When we finally completely unite with Him and become one with Him at the marriage of the Lamb, we will experience greater ecstasy than anything we can imagine. We may think marriage, family, sex, parenting, or human love on earth are wonderful, but just wait until we experience *echad*—oneness—with the One who created these things!

## A Longing Husband

The Lord longs for the consummation of our marriage to Him at the marriage supper of the Lamb. Yeshua is waiting in excited anticipation for the day He can have His bride. We find evidence of this in end-time prophecies throughout both the Old and New Testaments. For example, in the Book of Hosea the prophet relayed Jesus' excitement at the coming union with us:

> "It will come about in that day," declares the LORD,
> "that you will call Me Ishi [Husband] and will no
> longer call Me Baali [Master]....I will betroth you to
> Me forever; yes, I will betroth you to Me in righ-
> teousness and in justice, in lovingkindness and in
> compassion, and I will betroth you to Me in faith-
> fulness. Then you will know the LORD."
>
> —HOSEA 2:16, 19–20, NASB

On the glorious wedding day of the Lamb we will exchange calling Yeshua our master—or what in Hebrew is *Baali*, referring to the false god of Baal—for calling Yeshua *Ishi*, meaning "my husband."[3] In this verse the Lord was actually reproaching His people for addressing Him with the same formal religiosity they used in their sinful idol worship. He wanted to be close to them, and He was reminding them that the nature of their relationship was as close as that of a husband and wife.

The prophet Isaiah, who was a contemporary of Hosea, echoed this same idea: "For your Maker is your husband, the LORD of Hosts is His name" (Isa. 54:5).

Of course, God will still be our master; when we unite with Him we will not become God. But in the same way Jesus said, "I no longer call you servants....But I have called you friends" (John 15:15), we will become partners with the Lord, even ruling with Him in His kingdom. When we return to earth following the marriage supper of the Lamb, we will truly be partners in reigning with Him for all eternity. (See Revelation 20:6.) As Paul said, "If we endure, we shall also reign with Him" (2 Tim. 2:12).

Notice how the idea of progressive revelation, which we

addressed in an earlier chapter, is at work once again in the B'rit Hadashah (New Testament). The marriage between God and His people, which was unveiled in part in the Tanakh (Old Testament), is expanded with greater revelation through Yeshua HaMashiach in the New Testament. Can you see the thread connecting the Hebrew prophets we have already quoted to other parts of the New Testament? For example, in 2 Corinthians 11:2 Paul once again alludes to a heavenly marriage when addressing the believers in Corinth: "For I am jealous over you with godly jealousy. For I have espoused you to one husband, that I may present you as a chaste virgin to Christ."

John the Baptist understood the notion of Christ as the church's husband so much that He referred to himself as a "friend of the bridegroom" (John 3:29). And of course Jesus Himself frequently used the same marriage terminology to describe both His kingdom and His relationship with His church. Isn't it fascinating that in Matthew 25, out of all the analogies He could have used to portray His kingdom and His return, the Lord chose marriage? His parable of the ten virgins presents a perfect picture of how we are to prepare for the Bridegroom's arrival.

Although we already examined this parable earlier, I want to highlight one more thing from this rich passage that is particularly relevant to our times. More than two thousand years ago Jesus spoke of virgins waiting on a bridegroom who was taking much longer than they had anticipated. Even though Yeshua said only the Father knows the exact hour of His return (Matt. 24:36), He still knew human nature. He knew that we rarely like to wait on things, and that when we wait, we can get easily distracted or fall asleep. The virgins in Jesus' parable all went to sleep while waiting (Matt. 25:5), just as His own disciples fell asleep when He needed their support and prayer the most before going to the cross (Matt. 26:40–41).

So Jesus knew He needed to speak specifically to this issue of waiting, and His words are as if He were winking at us thousands of years in advance. He knew His return would probably take longer than most expected because He was aware of the condition of His church—and of the hearts of mankind. He left us with a specific word of warning to be ready no matter how long we had to wait because He knew that would be our greatest struggle. Sleep comes naturally when you are waiting for something or not expecting anything to happen. This is why Jesus cautioned us in Matthew 25:13 that we must not lose focus on Him while His return is delayed.

Two thousand years after Yeshua left for heaven we are still waiting for Him to return. And in many ways the church has been asleep for years. We must wake up and remain alert if we hope to be ready for His arrival. Two millennia ago Jesus warned us not to let the time delay between His first and second comings cause us to stop looking for Him, expecting His return, or cultivating our love for Him. We must keep the fires of our love burning, just as the wise virgins kept their lamps burning. When the bridegroom delayed in Jesus' parable, the entire group stopped looking for him. They became lethargic and fell asleep. But the wise virgins, despite resting, were still ready for his arrival at the midnight hour.

Think about it: What are most people doing at midnight? They are sleeping! In general, the only people not sleeping at midnight are those who have forced themselves to stay awake; they have been intentional about keeping themselves up.

Beloved, staying awake for our coming Bridegroom is not easy. We must be intentional about keeping ourselves alert. We must cultivate our love for the Lord and do whatever it takes to keep our fires of passion for Him burning. We must fight the natural tendency to get sucked into spiritual lethargy, apathy, or sleep.

The primary reason most believers fall into these things is not because of the enemy of our souls (Satan), though he will undoubtedly try to derail and distract us in our waiting. No, the primary reason is that we are not as intimate with Jesus right now as we need to be.

## CALLED OUT OF RELIGION AND INTO RELATIONSHIP

If we hope to be ready for the Lord's return, we must know Him and understand His heart. And those things come only through real relationship. Earlier in this chapter we discussed how God is a God of relationship. Religion is not relationship; religion is going through rituals out of duty. Beloved, God is not religious (in fact, much of Scripture proves He detests religious activity); He is relational. He called His people out of the bondage of Egypt and into the freedom of a relationship with Him. In the same way He is calling each of us into a deeper, more intimate relationship with Him. If you are not sure what that means or even looks like, then think about your most precious relationship on earth. How did that develop?

When I married my wife, Cynthia, in 1983, I was very selfish and didn't know how to sacrifice for her, be sensitive to her, or love her in a biblical way. Complicating this was the fact that she and I come from very different backgrounds and have different personalities. I am Jewish, and my wife is Gentile, and our cultural upbringings were anything but alike. I was not naturally open, so sharing my feelings with her was something I struggled with early in our marriage.

Paul said, "All things are exposed when they are revealed by the light, for everything that becomes visible is light" (Eph. 5:13). How I wish I had taken this verse more to heart in those early years! When I did not open up to Cynthia about the things that kept me in bondage, those very things continued to have power over me and kept me bound. But once I began sharing with her and brought those issues into the light, through the communication process they eventually fell off.

This did not happen naturally, nor did it happen overnight. It took surrendering my prideful, selfish ways and making an effort to communicate, keep myself open, and remain vulnerable to my wife. It involved dying to my old self, but the reward was worth it: Cynthia and I began to grow closer, and our intimacy and love increased. By learning how to die to myself and not insisting on my own way, I developed a greater level of appreciation, respect, and love for her. I became sensitive to her and realized some of her ways were better than my ways.

Today Cynthia and I have been married over forty years. The longer I am married to my wife, the more I get to know her, the more I love her, and the more intimate and beautiful our relationship becomes.

This is how it can be in our relationship with Jesus, only infinitely better. True love demands sacrifice and grows over time. The difference between the world's love and God's love is that the world's version is based on sexual attraction, which always fades. Yet love that is based on truth, commitment, and sacrifice always grows. Our earthly marriages will continue to flourish when we follow Jesus' pattern for love.

Of course, this applies to our relationship with Jesus our Bridegroom. Jesus said, "It is more blessed to give than to receive" because giving produces love (Acts 20:35). The more we give ourselves to Him, the more our love for Him grows. And as we prepare ourselves for meeting Jesus through the sacrifice of our obedience to Him, we can truly become those who have washed our garments and made ourselves ready for Him. (See Ephesians 5:26–27; Revelation 19:7–8.)

A day is coming when our *echad* with God will reach its climax. The oneness we have with Jesus will be expressed on every level—spiritual, physical, emotional, and likely in dimensions we have yet to discover. One day we will go from being betrothed to Yeshua to actually being married to Him. As we have seen, the Torah describes this marriage from its first pages. Moses continued to write about it throughout the first five books of the Hebrew Bible. Isaiah then wrote about it. Ezekiel and Hosea wrote about it.

This marriage relationship comes into greater clarity in the B'rit Hadashah through the words of Jesus, John the Baptist, Paul, and other New Testament writers. One day we will see the likes of Abraham, Isaac, Jacob, and all God's children celebrating this marriage and shouting: "Let us be glad and rejoice and give Him glory, for the marriage of the Lamb has come, and His wife has made herself ready" (Rev. 19:7).

CHAPTER 9

# ALL ISRAEL WILL BE SAVED

MANY YEARS AGO I had a dream about Israel, before I had ever set foot in the land. I dreamed I was floating in outer space and looking back at the earth, much like an astronaut would view it on a satellite or lunar mission. The view of the planet was stunning, but in this dream something was different. A mile-high pillar protruded from the top of the earth, right at its point of axis. This pillar was massive both in height and width. Sitting on top of the pillar was the nation of Israel. It was elevated above the rest of the earth, and as I gazed at this scene I felt God's glory flooding every particle of my being. In my spirit I sensed the Lord saying, "Israel isn't just a place where the prophets used to walk; it is still the place where I am. I am connected to that land like no other place on earth."

There is truly no nation like Israel on earth. God has made a unique, everlasting covenant with the Jewish people. His heart beats for His chosen people. Throughout the Bible we see Israel as the centerpiece of God's plans on earth, and this will continue in the last days. In the Book of Revelation, John often alludes to the Jewish people in his account and, in fact, spends much of chapter 7 identifying the specific number from each Israeli tribe that will be "sealed" by God (Rev. 7:3–8). Indeed Israel can be considered the very clock by which the end-times events run.

Yet perhaps one of the greatest miracles associated with

the Lord's return is what Paul declared about the Jewish people in Romans 11:25–27:

> For I do not want you to be ignorant of this mystery, brothers, lest you be wise in your own estimation, for a partial hardening has come upon Israel until the fullness of the Gentiles has come in. And so all Israel will be saved, as it is written: "The Deliverer will come out of Zion, and He will remove ungodliness from Jacob"; "for this is My covenant with them, when I shall take away their sins."

Did you catch that? "All Israel will be saved." Not some. Not part of or most of. "All Israel will be saved." That means when Yeshua returns, every Jewish person on the planet will turn to Him as Lord and Savior. About 7.2 million Jews currently live in Israel, while more than 8.5 million live throughout the rest of the world.[1] So if Yeshua returned right now—without any changes to the Jewish population, which obviously is impossible—more than 15 million Jews would suddenly have to go from denying Yeshua as Savior to recognizing Him as the true Son of God. By numbers alone, this is no small feat.

Later in this chapter we will examine the mystery and miracle of how this will happen with so many people. But before we do, I want to point out what I believe is an equally challenging obstacle to the fulfillment of Paul's prophecy. Simply stated, the problem is this: Most of Israel is lost. The majority of Jewish people on the planet today not only reject Yeshua as HaMashiach (the Messiah), but they are also secular, non-religious Jews.[2] As a Jewish believer in Yeshua HaMashiach, I am in the extreme minority. Most

Jews would say that to be Jewish inherently means you are still waiting for the Messiah to come (even though most Jews are not looking for a literal Messiah since they are secular). So from a believer's perspective, it is easy to see that Israel is still spiritually lost. Out of the 7.2 million Jewish people in Israel, only about eight thousand adults have embraced Yeshua as Messiah, according to research published in *Jesus-Believing Israelis: Exploring Messianic Fellowships*.[3]

But that is not the only way Israel is lost. A large part of the nation is lost in that they truly, literally cannot find themselves. Let me explain.

## THE TEN LOST TRIBES OF ISRAEL

Jewish history is full of conflict among the twelve tribes of Israel. Although King David succeeded in uniting all twelve tribes during his reign, this unity was short-lived. Following his son Solomon's death, the tribes split into two kingdoms: the northern kingdom of Israel, with ten tribes, and the southern kingdom of Judah, with two tribes.

In 722 BC Assyria captured the northern kingdom of Israel, and its ten tribes were deported to the massive Assyrian kingdom and served in exile in what today is Afghanistan and Iran. (See 2 Kings 17:5–6.) During this time these ten tribes completely assimilated into Assyrian culture, inter-married, and began losing elements of their own identity.

While the remaining two tribes of Judah eventually returned to their homeland even after being exiled into Babylon two centuries later, the ten tribes of Israel never returned. They eventually dispersed throughout the world and lost their Jewish heritage to such a degree that today they are known as the ten *lost* tribes of Israel. This is why

ever since then, the word *Jew* has been used interchange-
ably to describe anyone of Hebrew descent. *Jew* comes from
the word *Judah*, or in Hebrew *Yehudi*, meaning "from the
tribe of Judah." Since Judah was by far the larger of the two
tribes that were not lost, the name Jew was adapted. Today
the vast majority of Hebrews alive come from these two
remaining tribes.

So what exactly happened to the ten northern tribes?
Although the answer to that question remains a mystery,
the legend of these ten lost tribes has continued throughout
Jewish history. Some of the people groups thought to have
descended from them range from Native Americans to
Japanese to Afghans to the Falashas of Ethiopia.[4] But the
reality is that after more than twenty-five hundred years,
finding all these people is virtually impossible.

Except for God. Time is no hindrance to Him. He has
said all Israel will be saved—including the ten lost tribes—
and so shall it be. Tracing people's Hebraic roots is not an
obstacle for the Lord either because of how He has established Jewish lineage.

Since the time of Abraham an Israelite's identity has been
determined by the seed of the male. In other words, the Lord
established early on that to be a Jew (in the way that term is
used today) simply means your father is Jewish. Although
there have been concessions made at different times allowing
the mother to determine a child's identity, the biblical standard is that the father's seed determines whether a child is
Jewish. In fact, being Jewish is first about lineage, not about
belief. This is evidenced by male Jewish children being circumcised into a relationship with God and Israel at only
eight days old.

For many today, being Jewish has little to do with whether one is practicing rabbinic Judaism. As previously stated, more than half of the global Jewish population today is secular and does not attend synagogue on a weekly basis, yet these people are still considered Jewish by the general Jewish community.[5] Even atheistic and agnostic Jews are recognized as Jews within the wider Jewish world. So you see, you do not make yourself Jewish or choose to be a Jew; you are simply born into it by nature of your ancestry.

Although tracing Jewish lineage can be extremely difficult for humans, God knows exactly where we come from and what our true ancestry is. In His eyes these "lost" tribes of Israel are not lost but simply scattered. Let me give an example of this.

Imagine that a Jewish man marries a Gentile woman. He is not a "practicing Jew," nor is he concerned about spiritual things, so he and his wife decide they will not make Judaism a major factor in their home. One day they have a son. Although they raise him in a completely secular, non-religious, non-Jewish environment, that does not change his identity; he is still a Jew. The son grows up living a completely non-Jewish life and eventually marries a Gentile woman, just as his father did. They also have a son, who is raised even more removed from his Jewish roots. In fact, they rarely ever talk about being Jewish and certainly do not push it on their son. Regardless, this would have no effect on the boy's identity; he would still be Jewish. Eventually, this boy grows up to be a man, and he too marries a Gentile woman. They also have a son, and this time their boy grows up without ever even hearing the word *Jew* mentioned at home. Let me ask you: Does this change his identity as a Jew?

Not one bit! Whether he is called a Jew by his family or not, he is one. And so it is with those descended from the ten lost tribes of Israel. They may be far removed from their Jewish roots. Without question, twenty-seven hundred years is a long time.

Their cultural identity may have been mingled, mixed, blended, and enveloped with other cultures throughout the hundreds of passing generations. They may be clueless to their Hebrew identity, but in God's eyes they still come from the seed of Israel. And when Jesus returns, they will be among those redeemed when Scripture says, "All Israel will be saved" (Rom. 11:26).

Every one of Israel's tribes has been "found" by God and always has been. That will not change in the end times. Revelation 7:4–8 clearly explains that twelve thousand from each of the twelve Jewish tribes will be represented among the Israelites "sealed" by the Lord's protection during the tribulation. Despite the Jews' lost heritage, God will still remember the seed from which they were born. This is why He made such promises as found in Jeremiah:

> I will be found by you, says the LORD, and I will turn away your captivity and gather you from all the nations and from all the places where I have driven you, says the LORD, and I will bring you back into the place from where I caused you to be carried away captive.
>
> —JEREMIAH 29:14

See, I will gather them out of all countries wherever I have driven them in My anger, and in My fury, and in great wrath; and I will bring them again to this

place, and I will cause them to dwell safely. And they
shall be My people, and I will be their God.

—JEREMIAH 32:37–38

The Lord made a similar promise through Ezekiel when
He commanded the prophet to bind two sticks together in a
prophetic act symbolizing how the two kingdoms—northern
Israel and its ten lost tribes, and the two southern tribes—
will become one again in the last days (Ezek. 37:16–17).

The Lord has not lost the ten tribes of Israel. In fact, one
day we will see them not only reemerge as the nation of
Israel, but we will also see them reunite with the southern
tribes of Judah and Benjamin as the two sticks are joined
together at Yeshua's return.

## MISSING THE FOCUS

Today it is exciting to hear more reports suggesting that certain people groups, many living in remote places, may be
descendants of the ten lost tribes. For example, some anthropologists and Jewish leaders affirm that many Ethiopian Jews
are legitimate descendants of the tribe of Dan.[6] Likewise, a
people called the Bnei Menashe who live in the mountainous
region along the border of India and Myanmar are believed
to be descendants of Manasseh.[7] In fact, these and a few
other groups are now living in the Holy Land.

I am thrilled that we are discovering more about Israel's
lost tribes. But I am also frustrated by how a renewed interest
in these lost tribes has created a sudden wave of individuals
claiming to be descendants of Israel yet having no substantial proof. A few people in my own Messianic congregation
have claimed God revealed to them that they are descended

from one of the ten lost tribes. Most have said this with inarguable fervency yet zero evidence other than "God told me." This poses a bit of a problem for a rabbi, as you can imagine.

Some of these cases may be legitimate. Because it is so difficult to prove a person's lineage to the ten tribes, the possibility always exists. But my problem is less with the issue of heritage and more with the reason behind their claims. I have found many of these people have identity issues and for whatever reason think if their family came from these lost tribes, they would somehow be more important or significant. Even if they do not feel this way, many of these believers become so caught up in a search for their Hebraic roots that being an Israelite becomes the main focus rather than Jesus.

The truth is, believers are chosen in the Lord, whether Jew or Gentile. Our chosen-ness is ultimately about being chosen *in Him*.

This is why the apostle Paul said, "There is neither Jew nor Greek" (Gal. 3:28) and that "He has called, not from the Jews only, but also from the Gentiles" (Rom. 9:24). In terms of salvation, there is no difference between a Jew rejecting Jesus and a Gentile rejecting Jesus. Both need Him equally as much. Both will stand before Him on Judgment Day. The only thing that will matter on that day is not whether they came from Jewish heritage but whether they are covered by the blood of the Lamb, Jesus Christ.

Paul essentially made the same point when he argued that if anyone could take pride in being a tried-and-true, full-blooded Jew, it was he. "I was circumcised the eighth day," he wrote, "of the stock of Israel, of the tribe of Benjamin, and a Hebrew of Hebrews; as concerning the law, a Pharisee;

concerning zeal, persecuting the church; and concerning the righteousness which is in the law, blameless" (Phil. 3:5–6).

Paul undeniably had the stock. Yet at the end of the day, none of his qualifications mattered in the light of his knowing God, which is why he could say:

> But what things were gain to me, I have counted these things to be loss for the sake of Christ. Yes, certainly, I count everything as loss for the excellence of the knowledge of Christ Jesus my Lord, for whom I have forfeited the loss of all things and count them as rubbish that I may gain Christ, and be found in Him.
>
> —PHILIPPIANS 3:7–9

Paul went so far as to consider his own credentials—which were impressive—as good as garbage compared to his "credentials" in Jesus. This was how much he realized Jesus was the focus, not him. Paul said in 1 Corinthians 2:2, "For I determined not to know anything among you except Jesus Christ and Him crucified." Were it not for Yeshua's work in his life, Paul would have nothing to brag about. "If I must boast," he said, "I will boast of the things which concern my weakness" (2 Cor. 11:30). Paul knew that when he was weak, Christ's power could become even more evident in his life (2 Cor. 12:9). And he understood that Yeshua was the One who had saved him, not His "Jewishness" or his works.

## THE MASTER'S PLAN UNVEILED

Many believers call Paul's letter to the believers in Rome a masterful theological doctrine on salvation, and it most certainly is. But let's not forget that it also reflects Paul's heart for his own people, the Jews, and is a plea for the Israelites to come to their Messiah.

In Romans 9 Paul expressed his grief over Israel's blindness and its refusal to accept Jesus as God's Son: "I have great sorrow and continual anguish in my heart. For I could wish that I myself were accursed from Christ for my brothers, my kinsmen by race, who are Israelites" (Rom. 9:2–4). Paul was willing to give up his own salvation if that meant Israel would be saved! Such was the incredible extent of his love for his people.

Paul's grief continued into Romans 10, in which he said, "My heart's desire and prayer to God for Israel is that they may be saved" (Rom. 10:1). And in the following chapter he continued to reveal that Israel's salvation was at the forefront of his mind. It is important for us to remember that after Paul's dramatic conversion experience he originally set out to preach the gospel to the Jews. In his mind, who could be better qualified, with more "Jewish" credentials, to preach to the Jewish people than he? Every Jew in Jerusalem knew Paul had once excelled in hunting down Yeshua's followers and persecuting them even to death. So if someone like Paul could attest to the reality of Yeshua as God's Son, then surely they would know that this gospel was for real. Surely he would lead thousands upon thousands to salvation!

Yet God had other plans. Paul recounted what happened: "When I returned to Jerusalem and was praying in the temple, I fell into a trance and saw Him saying to me, 'Hurry! Get out of Jerusalem immediately, for they will not receive your testimony concerning Me'" (Acts 22:17–18). He then began to explain to God—as if the Lord did not know—that because of his past, he could be an effective witness to preach the gospel to the Jews. Yet the Lord replied: "Depart, for I will send you far away to the Gentiles" (v. 21).

I imagine Paul's heart sank at that moment. He probably thought this did not make sense. After all, why would the Lord *not* want him preaching the gospel to the Jews? Yet not only was Paul obedient to the Lord's call for him to preach to the Gentiles, but he soon began to see the Master's masterful plan on how to eventually bring Israel to salvation. This plan is what Paul unfolded in Romans 11, which I encourage you to read for greater understanding of just how profound God's design is. Essentially it involves the following elements:

1. God sent Paul to the Gentiles.

2. God will use the Gentiles to provoke the Jewish people to jealousy. Paul clearly stated this in Romans 11:11: "So I say, have they [the Jewish people] stumbled so as to fall [to spiritual ruin]? Certainly not! But by their transgression [their rejection of the Messiah] salvation has come to the Gentiles, to make Israel jealous [when they realize what they have forfeited]" (AMP).

3. As Gentiles come into "the fullness" of their calling—both numerically and in a spiritual sense (Rom. 11:25)—by provoking the Jews to jealousy, a critical mass of Jewish people will come to salvation. We do not know exactly how many saved souls among the Jews will constitute a tipping point, but we do know there *will* be a tipping point. As this mass of Jewish people comes to faith, they will begin

to call upon the Lord to return. Jesus prophesied this in Matthew 23:39 when He told the
Jewish crowds adoring Him that He would
not return until they once again said, "*Baruch
haba b'shem Adonai*," which means, "Blessed is
He who comes in the name of the Lord."

4. Finally, Jesus will respond to the call of this
critical mass of Jews and return to earth.
When He returns, *all* Israel will see the
Messiah for who He is, and then "*all* Israel will
be saved" (Rom. 11:26, emphasis added). As
every Jewish person on the planet comes to
faith in Yeshua HaMashiach, Romans 11:15
will be completely fulfilled: "For if their rejection means the reconciliation of the world,
what will their acceptance mean but life from
the dead?" Indeed, it will be "life from the
dead" for the entire world when all Israel is
saved. As Paul said in Romans 11:12, "Now if
their [the Jewish people's] transgression means
riches for the world, and their failure means
riches for the Gentiles, how much more will
their fullness mean?"

## THE MYSTERY REVEALED

Paul called God's ultimate plan for the Jews a "mystery"
that had been previously hidden but was now revealed
(Rom. 11:25). God has used the "partial hardening" of Israel
for a time—a season that has now lasted more than two
thousand years—to extend an open invitation for the rest
of the world to know Him. What was originally a divine

relationship exclusive to one group of people chosen by God (the Jews) became available to every person on the earth. The Lord's plan is beyond genius!

God knew that by making the Jewish people jealous of the Gentiles' blessings through faith in Yeshua, only then would their eyes be opened and their salvation come. Paul was excited by what this meant, for if the non-Jewish world could be blessed by Israel's sin and unbelief, how much more would the blessing come when Israel believed.

Furthermore, whom will God use to fulfill the prophecy that "all Israel will be saved"? Those who once were excluded from His blessing! Only God could devise such a wonderful strategy to bless the entire world. As Paul himself concluded in Romans 11, "O the depth of the riches and wisdom and knowledge of God! How unsearchable are His judgments and unfathomable are His ways!" (v. 33).

## A MATTER OF CALLING

When people get a glimpse of this mystery, often the first question they ask is, "When? When will this happen? When will there be a tipping point that leads to all Israel being saved?"

That may be a natural response, but as we have already discovered, only the Lord knows when this tipping point will occur or how many Jewish salvations it takes to reach a critical mass in heaven. Although there are only about eight thousand believing Jewish adults in Israel, it is still exhilarating to think that what only a few years ago was seemingly impossible to find—a Jewish follower of Yeshua—has now become an entire movement of Jewish believers that many refer to as Messianic Judaism. The number of Jews saved around the world increases every year—and that is living proof that we are in the last days! So although we don't know exactly how many Jews must come to know the Lord before He returns, we do know that every believer on the planet is pivotal to reaching a critical mass. Who knows if the next Jewish person you or I lead to the Lord will tip the scales of heaven?

Paul provided some insight into the timing of Jesus' return and its relationship to Israel by using an unusual phrase rich in meaning in Romans 11:25: "For a partial hardening has come upon Israel until *the fullness of the Gentiles* has come in" (emphasis added). What is "the fullness of the Gentiles"? I mentioned earlier how this has to do with the numerical "fullness" of the maximum number of Gentile people entering into God's kingdom prior to Jesus' return. But there is another type of fullness meant here as well.

I believe the fullness Paul described also includes the unique calling upon all Gentiles to take part in God's masterful plan to reach the Jewish people. If you are a Gentile, you have the amazing privilege of presenting the good news of Jesus Christ to the very people to whom He was first sent. When the Gentile world begins to grasp this responsibility and relies upon the Holy Spirit's empowering to share the truth, I believe the world will see one of the most powerful revivals in history occur exclusively among God's first-covenant people.

This will certainly not be the world's biggest revival in terms of numbers—that's impossible, given the relatively minuscule Jewish population compared with the rest of the world. But this revival will be powerful nonetheless. After all, when Jewish hearts are awakened and subsequently respond by calling upon Jesus to return, this ultimately ushers in the second coming. Now that's power!

The bottom line for the church is clear: We will not reach the fullness of our calling on earth until we recognize that Jesus' return is inherently linked to Israel's salvation, which is inherently linked to our sharing the gospel with the Jewish people. We must tell them the good news! As Paul so eloquently said:

> How then shall they call on Him in whom they have not believed? And how shall they believe in Him of whom they have not heard? And how shall they hear without a preacher? And how shall they preach unless they are sent? As it is written: "How beautiful are the feet of those who preach the gospel of peace, who bring good news of good things!"
> —ROMANS 10:14–15

Every believer has been called by God to be the bearer of good news. Naturally we are to preach the gospel of Jesus Christ to everyone, but our calling as the church is to reach "the Jew first, and also...the Greek" (Rom. 1:16). These are not mutually exclusive—we preach to both Jew and Gentile— yet even Paul indicates the importance and distinction of sharing the gospel with Israel. If we long to see Jesus part the skies, ride in on the clouds, and set foot on the Mount of Olives once again, then we all must understand our role in this genius plan.

## WHEN MOURNING DAWNS

Let's not forget that Jesus will return when all hope seems to be lost for Israel. Paul's prophecy that "all Israel will be saved" will be fulfilled when Jesus returns to save Israel both spiritually and physically from the clutches of hell. As we studied in chapter 6, the scene at Armageddon will be terrifying for the Jewish people still alive. Most will think this is the Holocaust revisited, only worse because virtually every nation in the world will be attacking them on their own soil. They will be on the brink of extermination.

You would think, then, that the coming of a Savior would elicit unbridled joy among the Jewish people who are in the midst of Armageddon. In fact, you would expect this to spark a massive wave of praise and thanksgiving throughout the land. But once again the Tanakh (Old Testament) and B'rit Hadashah (New Testament) stand in perfect union in their portrayal of how Israel will actually respond. In Zechariah we find this prophecy:

> And I will pour out on the house of David and over those dwelling in Jerusalem a spirit of favor and supplication so that they look to Me, whom they have pierced through. And *they will mourn* over him as one mourns for an only child *and weep bitterly* over him as a firstborn. On that day the mourning in Jerusalem will be as great as that of Hadad Rimmon in the plain of Megiddo.
> —ZECHARIAH 12:10–11, EMPHASIS ADDED

And in Revelation we find the scene described from a different angle yet with many of the same elements:

> Look! He is coming with clouds, and every eye will see Him, even those who pierced Him. And all the

> tribes of the earth will mourn because of Him. Even
> so, Amen.
>
> —REVELATION 1:7

When the one Israel "pierced" through at Golgotha returns, the Israelites will not initially break into celebration but will instead begin mourning. Their grief will be almost uncontrollable as they wail for the two thousand years of suffering, pain, and separation from God that He never desired for them. They will experience a deep remorse over the hardness of their hearts and over generations of stubborn blindness. They will weep for their spiritual pride that Jesus railed against when He first appeared to them. Most of all, they will mourn for what they did to the very One who gave up His perfect, sinless life for them. They will sense the weight of their actions and mourn for the suffering they caused.

But they also will experience the love and presence of God like never before. At some point the tears will stop and the season of mourning will end. From the ashes of grief will arise a new relationship. For the first time they will all, as one nation, desire their Savior and embrace Him fully. They will welcome Him back with open arms. They will believe He is indeed who He said He was and that this Yeshua who once walked among them was and is truly the Son of God.

After years and years of waiting, the Lord will finally have the desire of His heart: to be intimate with His people and dwell with them for all eternity. When all Israel has been saved and has welcomed Yeshua HaMashiach, at last God will have a people who will be partners with Him in love.

# CHAPTER 10

# GOD'S JUDGMENTS AND REWARDS

MAYBE RICKY HOLLOWAY never saw the first speeding ticket sent to his home for driving almost 20 miles per hour over the speed limit. Or maybe he innocently missed his second and third tickets, even though his car was clocked at going 30 miles an hour over the limit both times. But after *fourteen* tickets were sent to the twenty-three-year-old's home in East London and remained unpaid—each for different radar-detected speeding violations over a four-month period—you could only conclude that Holloway thought if he just ignored the tickets, they would go away.

They didn't. Within months, justice caught up with Holloway as he faced almost fourteen thousand dollars in fines, a court date with a local judge, and a six-month suspension of his driver's license.[1]

But justice is not always so quick to arrive, is it? Sometimes it seems justice never shows up. Maybe you have your own story of getting pulled over for a broken taillight while a hazardous drunk driver sped by unnoticed as a cop lectured you on the side of the road. Or maybe a coworker took credit for your tireless work on a project and landed the big promotion while all you got was a lousy company coffee mug. Or maybe it was when a business competitor got a pass for cheating on its taxes while your business went under because it took your clients.

Whatever the scenario, we all wonder at times if there really is justice in the world. Why is it that so many evil people either succeed or simply do not get caught, while those who try to honor God often get stepped on, used, or overlooked? Where is the justice in that?

The Bible features many people who asked God the same question. King David admitted that he "envied the proud when I saw them prosper despite their wickedness" (Ps. 73:3, NLT). Job asked, "Why do the wicked prosper, growing old and powerful?" (Job 21:7, NLT). Habakkuk complained to the Lord, "Why do You look on those who deal treacherously, and hold Your tongue when the wicked devours the man who is more righteous than he?" (Hab. 1:13). And Malachi claimed that, "Those who do wickedness are built up; they even test God and escape" (Mal. 3:15).

If you have asked God similar questions, you are not alone. There is nothing wrong with asking God tough questions. But how you resolve the ultimate question of whether evil will one day run its course is of the utmost importance. If we truly believe that those who do wrong will never face the consequences of their actions—whether in this life or the one to come—then there is no justice in the universe. And if the universe has no system of reward or punishment for how people have conducted themselves during their time on earth, then God is unjust and justice does not exist.

Think about it: What kind of God would you be serving if it did not matter whether you spent your whole life trying to be faithful to His words or spent it killing a million people? If the fate of the priest who molested children for his entire career is the same as Mother Teresa's, then not only is God unjust, but also there would be no ultimate point to our actions in life, for they would have no lasting effect or consequence.

But God *is* just. There *is* justice in the universe. It is easy to look around at the evil that goes unchecked in this world and wonder where God is. Some of us may even doubt His justice at times. But not only do we know God is just through His Word, but we know also that one day we will all experience His justice. God will have the last word. There is a coming judgment day.

Hebrews 9:27 says, "It is appointed for men to die once, but after this comes the judgment." Paul quoted the prophet Isaiah when he wrote, "We shall all stand before the judgment seat of Christ. For it is written: 'As I live, says the Lord, every knee shall bow to Me, and every tongue shall confess to God.' So then each of us shall give an account of himself to God" (Rom. 14:10–12). And Jesus Himself warned us, "But I say to you that for every idle word that men speak, they will give an account on the Day of Judgment" (Matt. 12:36).

Today we use the term *judgment day* so flippantly we even describe high-stakes sports events using the apocalyptic reference. But no matter how much culture waters down the phrase, it does not change the reality behind it. God has an end-time plan, and it is not a fairy tale. Just as real as the rapture, Armageddon, or Jesus' return are, there *will* be a judgment day, as the Book of Revelation reveals. Let's look, then, at what this day is really about.

## First Resurrection, First Judgment

Most people do not realize the Bible actually describes two separate judgments, just as it describes two distinct resurrections of the dead. Although distinguishing between these is not the focus of this chapter, it is important to at least read what Scripture says about each one.

The first judgment is the same one the apostle Paul referred to in Romans 14:10 when he said, "We shall all stand before the judgment seat of Christ." This will occur shortly after the first resurrection of the saints, which is the rapture. As we discussed in chapter 5, I believe the rapture (when Jesus removes the church from the world) will take place when the last trumpet of God's judgment sounds. As Paul indicated, "In a moment, in the twinkling of an eye, at the last trumpet, for the trumpet will sound, the dead will be raised incorruptible, and we shall be changed" (1 Cor. 15:52).

John expanded on this in his end-times revelation:

> I saw the souls of those who had been beheaded for their witness of Jesus and for the word of God. They had not worshipped the beast or his image, and had not received his mark on their foreheads or on their hands. They came to life and reigned with Christ for a thousand years. The rest of the dead did not come to life until the thousand years were ended. *This is the first resurrection.* Blessed and holy is he who takes part in the *first resurrection.* Over these the second death has no power, but they shall be priests of God and of Christ and shall reign with Him a thousand years.
> —REVELATION 20:4–6, EMPHASIS ADDED

The first resurrection is the raising of all believers—"the dead in Christ" (1 Thess. 4:16), those martyred during the tribulation, and those taken up during the rapture (Rev. 20:4). Remarkably, six hundred years before John wrote this, the

Hebrew prophet Daniel also spoke of this first resurrection and judgment:

> There shall be a time of trouble such as never was since there was a nation even to that time [the tribulation]. And at that time your people shall be delivered....Many of those who sleep in the dust of the earth shall awake, some to everlasting life, but others to shame and everlasting contempt.
>
> —DANIEL 12:1–2

After Yeshua has quickly overcome His enemies and cleansed the earth of its wickedness, He will sit in a judgment seat appointed exclusively for the Messiah. Paul described this in 2 Corinthians 5:10: "For we must all appear before the judgment seat of Christ, that each one may receive his recompense in the body, according to what he has done, whether it was good or bad." Jesus will begin His thousand-year reign by serving as the great judge and sitting in a judicial seat to reward or punish those according to what they did with their lives.

## SECOND RESURRECTION, SECOND JUDGMENT

The Bible also records that a thousand years later there will be a second resurrection and a second, final judgment. Once again we turn to the Book of Revelation for John's detailed description:

> Then I saw a great white throne and Him who was seated on it. From His face the earth and the heavens fled away, and no place was found for them. And I saw the dead, small and great, standing before

God. Books were opened. Then another book was opened, which is the Book of Life. The dead were judged according to their works as recorded in the books. The sea gave up the dead who were in it, and Death and Hades delivered up the dead who were in them. And they were judged, each one by his works. Then Death and Hades were cast into the lake of fire. This is the second death. Anyone whose name was not found written in the Book of Life was cast into the lake of fire.

—REVELATION 20:11–15

John says that all will come before the Lord as "the dead, small and great" and are raised to life to stand before a great white throne. (How else will they *stand* if they aren't living again?) This second judgment will be based on two group-ings of books. The first set of books involves the deeds, thoughts, intentions, and actions of those who have not received Jesus as the atonement for their sin. The other book is called "the Book of Life" and contains the names of those who have received Jesus the Lamb as the atonement for their sin. As you can see, this issue of atonement—making repa-ration for a wrong—is the core issue for both groups, and it is why Jesus so often told people in the Gospels, "Your sins are forgiven." He was ultimately warning people that unless they believed He was who He said he was, they would die in their sinfulness.

This second resurrection is all about separating humanity into two classes: those who will die in their sin because they did not receive the Lord Jesus and thus will be judged for their sin and sent into the lake of fire, and those who did receive God's precious gift of forgiveness through His Son and thus will enter into heaven (Rev. 20:15).

## THE FEAR OF GOD

If you have made Jesus your Lord and Savior yet are still worried that your name may not be in the Lamb's Book of Life, it is important to ask yourself why. If what you sense is the fear of God, there is nothing wrong with this; in fact, a holy fear of God is good. Even Paul had a healthy balance of being assured in his salvation while also acknowledging the risk of being "disqualified" by ungodly living (1 Cor. 9:27). His fear of God kept him alert in his body, spirit, and soul, while his understanding of God's grace grounded him in the assurance that he was "once saved, always saved." Often people lean too far to one side or the other of this pendulum instead of realizing we must balance the two.

Peter urged us to be diligent and make our "calling and election sure" (2 Pet. 1:10). We do this by simultaneously recognizing the truth that we are loved, forgiven, and saved and having a healthy realization that one day we will stand before the Lord and either be taken into heaven or sent into the lake of fire. Paul charged us to "examine yourselves, seeing whether you are in the faith; test yourselves" (2 Cor. 13:5). Likewise, Jesus told us to "strive to enter through the narrow gate" (Luke 13:24). Why must we take such effort as to *strive*? Because "many...will try to enter and will not be able" (v. 24). Now, that reality can put the fear of God in us!

At times I feel very sure that I am going to heaven. But I will admit that other times I am so aware of my hateful thoughts, accusatory words, and selfish attitudes that I start to question whether I will go to heaven. This does not mean

I constantly go from being saved to being unsaved. I have always believed I am chosen, loved by God, and truly saved. But an awareness of my ongoing tendency to fall short of God's holiness leaves me in a posture in which I understand His mercy over my life while also fearing the reality of what would happen without such mercy. This is the fear of God, and it causes us to be afraid when we walk in sins such as hate, selfishness, or unforgiveness.

Solomon, the wisest man who ever lived, said, "The fear of the LORD is the beginning of knowledge" (Prov. 1:7, NIV). Psalm 111:10 said it "is the beginning of wisdom; all who live it have insight." A healthy fear of God leads us into godly living by shining a light on our path, keeping us from making poor decisions that will harm us.

Some of you can relate to this kind of fear by thinking of your relationship with your earthly parents. Growing up, you knew they loved and cherished you, but you also knew that if you did certain things, you would be punished. Their punishment did not come out of a desire for them to inflict harm upon you but instead out of their love to see you flourish and make the right choices.

The same is true with God. Part of fearing Him involves not living a life of willful sin. Yeshua said bluntly, "Do not fear those who kill the body but are not able to kill the soul. But rather fear Him who is able to destroy both soul and body in hell" (Matt. 10:28). Remember, God "does not want any to perish" (2 Pet. 3:9). He desires for us to "enter through the narrow gate" into heaven (Luke 13:24). How, then, do we "strive" to enter through this gate, as Jesus told us to do? By continually repenting. Jesus said, "Repent! For the kingdom of heaven is at hand" (Matt. 4:17) and that unless we repent, we will perish (Luke 13:5). How do we truly repent? We continually examine our thoughts, attitudes, and actions. We ask ourselves whether we are abiding in Christ, denying ourselves to follow Him, and being conformed to His image, or whether we are living self-willed, selfish, and independent lives. This does not mean we are perfect but that we are on an upward journey toward perfection. It means we truly desire to please God and that we are growing in Christlikeness.

Yeshua said, "If anyone wishes to come after Me, he must deny himself, and take up his cross daily and follow Me. For whoever wishes to save his life will lose it, but whoever loses his life for My sake, he is the one who will save it" (Luke 9:23–24, NASB). Simply saying a prayer at a church service is not enough. We must die to ourselves daily and follow Jesus if we want to find our names written in the Book of Life. As we continually yield to the Lord, we will "reassure our hearts before Him" and gain confidence that we will indeed go to heaven (1 John 3:19).

The Book of Life should cause each of us to consider eternity with the utmost gravity. If what you sense as you read these pages is a healthy fear of God, understand that the Holy Spirit is working inside of you. But if what you sense is more condemning than just a holy fear, allow me to remind you of the good news.

Romans 3:10 says, "There is none righteous, no, not one." In fact, Isaiah 64:6 says, "All our righteousness is as filthy rags." Nothing we could ever do will make us righteous or clean enough before God to warrant our names being recorded in the Book of Life. We cannot work our way into eternity with the Lord. There is only one thing that gets us into this supreme book: being washed by the blood of the Lamb, Yeshua HaMashiach.

Just as at Passover the only thing that saved a person was the blood of a perfect, spotless lamb, so it will be when the Book of Life is opened. True believers know they have done nothing to deserve eternal life; it is simply because of the perfect, spotless Lamb of God and His work in their lives.

## COMING WITH REWARDS

In Revelation 22:12 Jesus tells His followers, "Look, I am coming soon! My reward is with Me to give to each one according to his work." It is crucial that we realize Jesus is not just coming to judge, but He is also coming to reward. Keep in mind these are not unlimited "freebies" but are rewards based entirely on what we have done during our time on earth.

I hear very few preachers touch this subject today, in part because most do not want to be accused of promoting a works-based faith. It is far more common to hear sermons on grace than on the topic of our heavenly rewards. I wonder, however, if the pendulum has not swung too far to the other extreme. After all, there are dozens of scriptures speaking of these rewards—yes, including works-based ones—throughout the Bible. In the Tanakh, for example, we find the following (I have put specific references to these rewards in italics):

> See, the Lord GOD will come with a strong hand, and His arm shall rule for Him; see, His *reward* is with Him, and His *recompense* before Him.
> —ISAIAH 40:10

The LORD has proclaimed to the ends of the earth: Say to the daughter of Zion, "See, your salvation comes; see, His *reward* is with Him, and His *recompense* before Him." They shall call them The Holy People, the Redeemed of the LORD; and you shall be called Sought Out, a City Not Forsaken.

—ISAIAH 62:11–12

The LORD *rewarded* me according to my righteousness; according to the cleanness of my hands He has *repaid* me.

—PSALM 18:20

People will say, "Surely there is a *reward* for the righteous; surely there is a God who judges on the earth."

—PSALM 58:11

Now compare those Old Testament verses with some of their New Testament counterparts:

For the Son of Man shall come with His angels in the glory of His Father, and then He will *repay* every man according to his works.

—MATTHEW 16:27

Blessed are you when men revile you, and persecute you, and say all kinds of evil against you falsely for My sake. Rejoice and be very glad, because great is your reward in heaven, for in this manner they persecuted the prophets who were before you.

—MATTHEW 5:11–12

> Now he who plants and he who waters are one, and each one will receive his own *reward* according to his own labor.
>
> —1 CORINTHIANS 3:8

> From now on a *crown* of righteousness is laid up for me, which the Lord, the righteous Judge, will give me on that Day, and not only to me but also to all who have loved His appearing.
>
> —2 TIMOTHY 4:8

And then there are verses such as the following that, while not specifically mentioning rewards, definitely allude to what awaits us—and how that is connected to what we do on earth.

> But as it is written, "Eye has not seen, nor ear heard, nor has it entered into the heart of man the things which God has prepared for those who love Him."
>
> —1 CORINTHIANS 2:9

> "Let us be glad and rejoice and give Him glory, for the marriage of the Lamb has come, and His wife has made herself ready. It was granted her to be arrayed in fine linen, clean and white." Fine linen is the righteous deeds of the saints.
>
> —REVELATION 19:7–8

And finally, Jesus' words from the last chapter in the Bible:

> Look, I am coming soon! My reward is with Me to give to each one according to his work.
>
> —REVELATION 22:12

We will be rewarded as God brings all things into the light at the judgment seat of Elohim—every act, every thought, every word, every deed, every intention. Again, Paul said we will "all appear before the judgment seat of Christ, that each one may receive his recompense in the body, according to what he has done, whether it was good or bad" (2 Cor. 5:10). When you really think about it, this has profound meaning, doesn't it? It means *everything* matters! What we do while we have bodies does not just impact today, tomorrow, next year, or even a few years from now; it determines what will happen when we die! Simply stated, how we live our lives has eternal consequences. The apostle Paul declared:

> There is one glory of the sun, and another glory of the moon, and another glory of the stars. One star differs from another star in glory. So also is the resurrection of the dead....Therefore, my beloved brothers, be steadfast, unmovable, always abounding in the work of the Lord, knowing that your labor in the Lord is not in vain.
>
> —1 Corinthians 15:41–42, 58

## Greater Motivation

As we are beginning to see, Scripture is clear that what we do now determines what we will do and receive in heaven. What we work toward here on earth determines what rewards we will receive at the Lord's judgment seat, and these rewards last *forever*.

This alone should awaken us to live life with purpose and a greater goal. It changes our entire motivation. It affects how we approach our job, how we spend our money, how we treat our spouse. It changes our perspective on whether we're being faithful to the Lord as a true witness for Him and sharing His love with others. It causes us to consider whether we are actually growing our love for Him or just coasting on past encounters. And it is also why Jesus encouraged us with the ultimate reminder:

> Do not store up for yourselves treasures on earth where moth and rust destroy and where thieves break in and steal. But store up for yourselves treasures in heaven, where neither moth nor rust destroy and where thieves do not break in nor steal, for where your treasure is, there will your heart be also.
> —MATTHEW 6:19–21

He also reminded us that Elohim sees all things. He recognizes even the smallest things we do in private that please Him, and He will not forget these when judgment day comes. Yeshua encouraged us to keep this in mind particularly in our prayer life.

> When you pray, you shall not be like the hypocrites. For they love to pray standing in the synagogues and on the street corners that they may be seen by men. Truly I say to you, they have their reward. But you, when you pray, enter your closet, and when you have shut your door, pray to your Father who is in secret. And your Father who sees in secret will reward you openly.
> —MATTHEW 6:5–6

The point is, the Lord judges by what goes on behind closed doors, not just by what is seen in public. We also know He looks at the heart and not just the outward appearance (1 Sam. 16:7). Because of these kingdom principles, Jesus said we will likely be surprised on judgment day by who will be rewarded most. Throughout the Gospels He talked about how "many who are first will be last, and the last first" (Matt. 19:30); how the greatest will be the least, and the least the greatest (Matt. 23:11); and how those who exalt themselves on earth will be humbled while the humble will be lifted up (v. 12). He told a detailed story about the surprising afterlife fates of a wealthy man and a beggar named Lazarus, and how their standings were turned around at death (Luke 16:19–31). If you have not already figured it out, these verses of Scripture were all talking about what will happen on judgment day!

We will be rewarded for everything we do for God, no matter how small it seems. For example, we will be rewarded for holding our tongue when we wanted to lash out with angry words, but instead of letting our flesh rule us, we chose to abide in the Holy Spirit out of our love for Him. The Lord will reward us for when we spent time with Him in prayer rather than in front of the television. He will remember every time we shared our faith with someone to be obedient to Him even though we were afraid. He will not forget the countless mornings when we awoke early to go to a job we did not like yet one where we served as His witness to others.

He sees when we have done all these things because we love Him and because we desire for Him to shape our lives according to His will. He sees when we have waited patiently on Him, or when we have responded to trials, suffering, or injustice with worship. All this matters. It *really* does!

## WHAT YOU DETERMINE

We cannot control everything in life. We cannot determine, for example, to whom we are born or what kind of heritage we have. You may have come from a home in which you did not have a mother or father around—or even if parents were around, maybe they were not good parents. You may have come from a background with limited opportunities, from a family that did not value education or one that lacked enough money to send you to college. You may be able to point to circumstances in your life as the reasons you have not ended up in the place you thought or hoped you would.

These are things none of us can control. But we *can* control where we will be in the life to come. In fact, you are the *only* person who determines what you will be doing in the millennial kingdom where Jesus will reign for a thousand years. Your family, work, finances, marriage, education— none of that affects the rewards we have been talking about. You will not be able to blame anyone for the position you have in the life to come. Regardless of what you have or do not have in this life, you can receive an abundance when the Messiah gives out His rewards. What we do and where we will be in God's eternal kingdom will be determined by how much we obey the Lord and put Him first in our lives during our time on this earth.

Nicholas Herman was born into a poor family in France sometime between 1605 and 1614. His surroundings were so meager that we do not even know the exact date of his birth, likely because no one expected him to live or, if he did live, to amount to much. He had no chance of receiving an education and could not get a job. So after being wounded as a soldier, he entered into a community of monks in Paris called the Carmelite Order, where he took on the name Brother Lawrence. Even there his past limited him; because he lacked education, he could not become a cleric and, as a lowly lay brother, was assigned to kitchen duty. Every day he was responsible for preparing food, washing dishes, and mopping floors.[2]

He did not like this. But four centuries later we know Brother Lawrence not for how he enjoyed his work but for how he used it to serve God to his fullest. His conversations, letters, and journal entries were compiled into the now-classic book *The Practice of the Presence of God*, in which he writes: "We ought not be weary of doing little things for the love of God, who regards not the greatness of the work, but the love with which it is performed."[3]

If all we are doing is chasing rewards in heaven, we have missed the point. The end goal is not just how many eternal rewards we can accumulate, even though it is good and wise for us to keep these rewards in mind. But far, far surpassing any of our rewards will be the eternal reward of Jesus Himself. He is the One we must treasure and pursue. We make the most of our life on earth by being passionate about Him, not about what we can get after we die. When He remains our focus, the rest takes care of itself. His presence will be enough—in fact, it will be total ecstasy.

At the judgment seat of Christ many of the big-name preachers, self-proclaimed prophets, and hyped apostles will likely take a backseat to the janitors, cooks, and groundskeepers who served in their ministries yet did it all "unto the Lord." Years ago Bible teacher Rick Joyner had a series of visions that illustrated the same point. In his book *The Final Quest* he shared a vision of heaven in which he saw people shining with different degrees of light and glory. He was shocked because many of the people he recognized from earth with major ministries, high-profile positions, and big audiences shone with a glory much dimmer than those who lived simpler lives—those who had been faithful in their "simple" roles as secretaries, teachers, husbands, mothers, or neighbors.[4]

Less important than *what* you are doing right now is *whom* you are doing it for and *why*. Whether you are responsible for preaching the Word of God in a crowded church or serving as a construction worker, nurse, salesperson, or dentist, it makes little impact on your standing in Jesus' kingdom to come. But what will determine your position is whether you do those things with a heart full of love and service toward Him. This is why we must continue to make cultivating our relationship with Him the primary objective of our life.

## PLEASURE NOW OR LATER

In the 1960s a Stanford psychologist named Walter Mischel studied the response of more than six hundred children in a now-famous experiment called "the marshmallow test." Mischel would bring each child into a room containing a single treat (usually a marshmallow) on a table. He would offer the child a deal: "You can eat the treat now, or if you can resist eating it for the next fifteen minutes, I'll come back and reward you with two treats." Then he would leave the room.[5]

The video footage of these children, aged four to six, was entertaining in itself. Mischel certainly found out some interesting things about children, self-control, and delayed gratification. But it was the follow-up studies of these children over the next forty years that brought the true discovery. Mischel and other researchers recognized that the children who had been willing to wait for a second treat ended up doing better in almost every area of life. Their grades and test scores were higher. They were less likely to abuse substances or become obese. They responded to stress better and showed more advanced social skills.[6] The bottom line of their findings: The ability to delay gratification is a key part of succeeding in life.

Jesus said the same thing in urging us to be more concerned with storing up heavenly treasures than amassing the riches of the earth (Matt. 6:19–21), as we read earlier. The Lord desires to position us for eternal glory and blessings that last forever. But the degree to which we will enjoy future rewards with Him rests upon our ability to delay gratification now. Can we say no to the things of this world grabbing for our affections, our attention, and our very life? Can we crucify our "flesh with its passions and lusts," as Paul described (Gal. 5:24)? Can we endure momentary suffering while keeping our eyes fixed on the bigger prize of eternity with Jesus?

The choice is up to us and no one else. Meanwhile the opportunity to make the right decision and store up heavenly treasures presents itself throughout each day. We live in a constant battle between two worlds—the kingdom of light and the kingdom of darkness—each vying for our eternity. Satan would like nothing more than to rob us of the eternal rewards awaiting us with Jesus. He wants to see us destroyed. God, on the other hand, wants to bless us. Jesus said that the thief comes "to steal and kill and destroy," but that He came "that they may have life, and that they may have it more abundantly" (John 10:10).

Until Yeshua returns, we will continue to see this battle waged on the earth. It reminds me of a recent trip I took to the Columbus Zoo and Aquarium in Ohio. The night was cold and snowy, and the zoo had a special light display for the Christmas season. Everywhere I walked it was like a winter wonderland, with beautiful blues and greens shining all around. The spectacular beauty continued as my family and I ventured into the aquarium, where I was in awe of God's creative imagination. Fish of every imaginable color swam in crystal-clear water. Every hue and shade seemed to be represented and sparkled on the glittery fish scales—vibrant yellows, dazzling reds and oranges, deep purples, mesmerizing blues and greens. As I took in the Lord's beauty, I could feel His presence and glory—yes, even at the Columbus Zoo.

A few minutes later we walked into the building where reptiles are kept, and I suddenly felt the exact opposite. I have been around reptiles before and have never had an aversion to them, but this time I was repulsed by what I saw. I felt sick and wanted to leave the building as soon as I could. The lizards, snakes, and turtles were all covered in drab, colorless tones—ugly browns and grays. The air smelled foul, and everywhere I looked it seemed as if life had been emptied, as a snake sheds a layer of its dead skin. I now believe this was a prophetic experience.

Once outside I was reminded of how the earth contains both kingdoms, symbolized in this experience to me by the beautiful, colorful, kosher fish on the one hand and the dark, ugly, unkosher reptiles on the other. In this world are both the kingdom of God and light, and the kingdom of Satan and darkness. We can choose between these two spiritual kingdoms that coexist here on this earth. The Lord said, "I have set before you life and death, blessing and curse. Therefore choose life, that both you and your descendants may live" (Deut. 30:19).

Earth is the only place in the universe where God's kingdom coexists—for a time—with Satan's. It is up to us which kingdom we choose to be part of, and that is not just a one-time decision. Every day we make choices that affect where we are "laying up" our treasures. Are we storing things in God's kingdom of light by what we do publicly and privately, in a kingdom of vibrant colors and life abundant, where things last forever? Or are we participating in Satan's kingdom, which will soon turn to ashes?

One kingdom is on its way out and will be wiped away upon Messiah's return; the other has come and continues to expand. So which will it be?

In the last chapter of the entire Bible Yeshua reminds us that He is coming soon and that when He arrives, He will reward "each one according to his work" (Rev. 22:12). As unpopular as it may be today to emphasize these rewards, I believe it is crucial that we start living with the right perspective—namely an eternal one. Our lives on earth are but a flash in the pan compared with eternity on the other side of judgment day. And yet what we do right now—for good or for bad—matters forever. The Lord will return. He will judge. And He will reward. I pray this truth provides you with a godly motivation to live your life with greater purpose and to love the only One who matters in the long run.

# CHAPTER 11

# THE REALITY OF HELL

I AM OLD ENOUGH to remember when *hell* was still a bad word. When I was in elementary school, I knew that if I dared let the word slip from my mouth, my teachers would strongly rebuke or discipline me. No one wanted to face the wrath of our teachers, and so we all thought of *hell* as a curse word never to be spoken aloud. But when I was eight or nine years old, I remember encountering someone who didn't exactly share this view.

My family belonged to a country club at the time, and during the summer that's where we would swim and hang out for hours. While the kids played in the water, the grown-ups drank and socialized. I will never forget one man in particular, who was always loud and boisterous and did not require any alcohol to spice up his language. As the adult conversation grew louder and rowdier, I could hear this man often use the word *hell* as he laughed. Though others laughed along and were drawn to his outgoing personality, it was still unusual—and offensive—to hear the word spoken so casually in public.

Times have certainly changed! Today even believers sometimes use the word *hell* flippantly in everyday conversations. People now use *hell* to describe how they feel, how something tastes, how something looks, or even how their day was.

As much as the use of *hell* in our language has digressed, that may pale in importance when compared with our culture's shifting perception of what hell really is. According to a recent Pew Research poll, 62 percent of Americans believe hell is an actual place.[1] Two decades ago that number was 70 percent,[2] meaning in less than twenty years millions of people went from acknowledging hell as a reality to saying it is nothing more than a fairy tale.

Ask Bill Wiese if hell is just a myth. He and his wife were plugging away at their careers as real estate brokers until everything changed on November 23, 1998, when he was suddenly awakened from his sleep at three in the morning and transported into hell. For the next twenty-three minutes he experienced the reality of hell with all his senses. His riveting account, shared in the *New York Times* best-selling book *23 Minutes in Hell*, details everything from hell's putrid smells to its constant, overwhelming heat to the sound of billions crying out in agony and utter loneliness.

Wiese says his journey was not a dream or near-death experience but a physical visitation to hell granted by the Lord. He had never taken drugs, watched horror movies, or done anything that might trigger such an incident. He is by nature very conservative and, though he had been a believer for almost three decades at that point, had never studied or even thought much about hell. In short, he was an unlikely candidate for this experience. And yet the harrowing visit impacted him so much he immediately began traveling around sharing his story—something he promised the Lord he would do—and soon quit his job to minister full time.[3]

Of course, the first thing most people do when they hear Wiese's story is question its validity. He understands that and has gone to great lengths since he began speaking in 1999 to prove his story is not fabricated, including lining up his account with more than two hundred scriptures. But of far greater concern to Wiese than what people think of his story is the number who think hell itself is just a contrived concept.

"When you know the truth, you want so desperately to convince others that hell is real and that Jesus is their only way out," Wiese says. "It is not just that I am anxious to talk to others because of my experience—it's also because of what God says in His Word. That is what counts."[4]

What God's Word says about hell is indeed the ultimate truth, and yet countless people—including believers—refuse to accept what the Bible says about hell, much less the accounts of those who say they have been there. Satan continues to use such stubborn unbelief and deception to keep these people in the dark and ultimately on the path to unending misery. It is part of his current plan, and it will also be part of his end-time strategy as he attempts to take as many people as possible with him to hell. So as we continue examining the Book of Revelation through the eyes of the Hebrew prophets, let's take an extensive look at how the reality of hell is revealed in both the Old and New Testaments, and how it factors into the end times.

## ACCEPTED REALITY

In Revelation 14:9–11 hell is presented as the consequence for all who receive the mark of the beast in the last days:

> A third angel followed them, saying with a loud voice, "If anyone worships the beast and his image and receives his mark on his forehead or on his hand, he also shall drink of the wine of the wrath of God, which is poured out in full strength into the cup of His anger. He shall be tormented with fire and

brimstone in the presence of the holy angels and in the presence of the Lamb. The smoke of their torment will ascend forever and ever. They have no rest day or night, who worship the beast and his image and whoever receives the mark of his name."

From this we see that hell is inherently connected to God's wrath, which is associated with being "tormented with fire and brimstone" that lasts "forever and ever," with "no rest day or night." But many people today refuse to connect this passage and others in Revelation with hell since the word is never specifically mentioned, and they use this as proof that hell is merely an allegory rather than an actual place. They avoid the reality of hell like much of the Jewish community today. Despite the reality of hell being so foundational in the ancient Jewish Scriptures, I have never once heard a traditional rabbi talk about hell in all my years of living.

When I was growing up in a conservative Jewish community, the only thing I heard mentioned about the afterlife was that those who die "go to a better place." Secular society has a similar worldview that hell does not exist and that everyone will instead go to "a happier place" when they die. Unlike in today's culture, however, hell was an accepted reality in both Old Testament and New Testament times, and the Hebrew Scriptures reveal it as a literal place.

The Bible contains far too many mentions of hell (or what was often referred to as "Sheol," "Hades," "the grave," or "the pit") to list here—roughly one hundred fifty in all.[5] Most of the ancient Hebrew prophets spoke of hell, including the likes of Moses, David, Solomon, Isaiah, Jeremiah, Ezekiel, Amos, Habakkuk, and Zechariah.

For example, Isaiah 38:18 says, "For Sheol cannot thank You, death cannot praise You; those who go down into the pit cannot hope for Your faithfulness." Job, the oldest book in the Hebrew Bible, contains several mentions of hell, including: "He will deliver his soul from going down to the pit" (Job 33:28). Psalm 9:17 says, "The wicked will be turned to Sheol, and all the nations that forget God." And David later wrote, "Great is Your mercy toward me, and You have delivered my soul from the depths of Sheol" (Ps. 86:13).

So clearly, the reality of hell is affirmed in the Old Testament. Likewise the Gospels are filled with mentions of hell. Jesus taught on the topic as much as He taught on heaven. In Mark 9:44 He went back and quoted Isaiah, validating the prophet's description that hell is where "their worm does not die, and the fire is not quenched." In Matthew 11:23 He promised that the unrepentant town of Capernaum "will be brought down to Hades."

Just two chapters later, in explaining His parable of the weeds, He said:

> Therefore as the weeds are gathered and burned in the fire, so shall it be in the end of this world. The Son of Man shall send out His angels, and they shall gather out of His kingdom all things that offend, and those who do evil, and will throw them into a fiery furnace. There will be wailing and gnashing of teeth.
> —MATTHEW 13:40–42

These scriptures barely scratch the surface of the Bible's mentions of hell. Considering there are one hundred fifty direct mentions or references to hell in the Old and New

Testaments,[6] one thing is clear: God's Word is definitive that hell is an actual, literal place, not some man-made myth.

## CORE LOCATION

If hell is a real place, then is it possible for us to know exactly where it is? I believe it is. People often find it difficult to imagine where hell is located, much less what it is like, because they are uncertain of what God's Word says or they think Scripture itself is not specific enough. But much to people's surprise, the Bible is actually very specific when it comes to hell's location. In fact, I believe it clearly describes hell as being in the center of the earth.

Let me explain. In some of the verses I have already referenced, hell is alluded to as being "down" or "beneath." This is true in dozens of other passages as well. In Psalm 55:15, for example, David wrote, "May death surprise them, and may their lives go down to Sheol, for wickedness is in their dwellings and among them." In Isaiah 14:9 the prophet said, "Hell from beneath is moved for you to meet you at your coming." In the Hebrew Bible (Old Testament), Sheol is often described as a pit, and people descend from the earth into this pit of fire, death, and darkness.

That hell is beneath the earth's surface is alluded to in an unusual occurrence in Moses's time, recorded in the Book of Numbers. At the time a man named Korah led a group of Israelite men in a coup not just against Moses and Aaron but ultimately against the Lord's leadership. Moses put a stop to their rebellion by making a bold promise to all the children of Israel that if the earth did not suddenly swallow these men, then he was not God's man. What happened next was remarkable:

> So it was, when he finished speaking all these words,
> that the ground that was under them split open. And
> the earth opened its mouth and swallowed them,
> and their houses, and all the men that belonged to
> Korah, and all their goods. And they and all that
> belonged to them went down alive into the pit, and
> the earth closed on them, and they perished from
> among the assembly.
>
> —Numbers 16:31–33

Why is this passage significant in our discussion of hell if it does not even mention the word? It's because "the pit" of verse 33 is a shadow of hell itself. Those who followed Korah fell into the pit and sank deep into the crevices of the earth. Because all of Israel witnessed this horrific scene in person, this was likely a milestone moment in Hebrew culture confirming the reality of hell's location. This is not poetic language; it is historical fact documented in the Torah.

When we examine many of the Bible's passages dealing with hell, we find similar and even more specific language indicating hell's location. In Psalm 63:9 David said, "Those who seek my soul to destroy it will go into *the lower parts of the earth*" (emphasis added). Ezekiel 31:14 says, "For they all have been delivered to death, to *the nether parts of the earth* in the midst of the sons of men, with those who go down to the pit" (emphasis added). And hundreds of years later Paul explained in his letter to the Ephesians the reality of what happened when Jesus died: "In saying, '[Yeshua] ascended,' what does it mean but that He also descended first into *the lower parts of the earth*?" (Eph. 4:9, emphasis added).

I do not believe this is coincidence, nor do I think these

men were using some generic, cliché phrase. I think they were giving us a key to understanding where hell is—a key we have since lost in our generation that barely believes hell exists!

Listen to how Ezekiel used this same phrase again in another description of hell:

> For thus says the Lord God: When I make you a desolate city, like the cities that are not inhabited, when I bring up the deep upon you and great waters shall cover you, then I shall bring you down with those who descend into the pit, to the people of old, and make you dwell *in the lower parts of the earth*, in places desolate of old, with those who go down to the pit so that you will not be inhabited.
> —Ezekiel 26:19–20, emphasis added

Did you catch something in the first part of that passage? The Lord said He would "bring up the deep upon you and great waters shall cover you" (v. 19). What are the deep and great waters Ezekiel mentions? The oceans! The earth's deepest locations are its ocean floors, which can lie as much as thirty-six thousand feet beneath sea level.[7] And what ultimately lies far beneath the ocean floors of the world? The center of the earth—a place with hellish temperatures!

Almost four thousand miles beneath the earth's surface exists the hottest place on the planet, with temperatures reaching an astounding *10,800 degrees* Fahrenheit.[8] The deepest humans have ever dug into the earth is a "mere" seven and a half miles, where the temperature reached 356 degrees.[9] Consider that the hottest temperature ever recorded on earth is 134 degrees, and that during the World

Trade Center attacks of September 11, 2001, people opted to jump out of windows and plunge to their deaths rather than face the eighteen-hundred-degree temperature inside the top floors.[10]

As terrible as those temperatures were, they pale when compared with those of hell. And if any location matches up with the Bible's consistent description of hell being a place with unceasing heat and fire, it is the core of the earth. Several times in the Gospels Jesus describes hell as having an "unquenchable" and "eternal" fire. (See Matthew 18:8; 25:41; Mark 9:43–48; Luke 3:17.) In the Book of Revelation, John compares the smoke rising from the bottomless pit of hell to "the smoke of a great furnace" (Rev. 9:2).

## A CONVERGENCE OF ACCOUNTS

We can hardly fathom the numbers associated with how deep and hot hell is. Yet before you think I am stretching my scriptural interpretation too far and mixing scientific fact with fiction, let me point out another remarkable correlation. Whether people believe the numerous accounts of individuals who say they have visited hell, it is impossible to deny the common threads among their accounts—of how these individuals got there and once there what it was like. Among the countless stories of people experiencing hell yet returning to tell about it, here are but a few that highlight the uncanny consistencies:

- Bill Wiese's time in Hades began with his being catapulted in the middle of the night and instantly plummeting downward into hell. Once there, he experienced heat, despair, hopelessness, loneliness, and pain of all forms that were infinitely worse than anything he had experienced on the earth.

"The very first thing I noticed was the temperature," he wrote. "It was hot—far beyond any possibility of sustaining life. It was so hot that I wondered, *Why am I still alive? How could I survive such intense heat? My flesh should disintegrate from off my body at any moment.* The reality was that it didn't. This wasn't a nightmare; it was real." [11]

Later Wiese became nauseated from the constant foul stenches in hell: "[They were], by far, the most putrid smells I have ever encountered. If you could take every rotten thing you can imagine, such as an open sewer, rotten meat, spoiled eggs, sour milk, dead rotting animal flesh, and sulfur, and magnify it a thousand times, you might come close. This is not an exaggeration. The odor was actually extremely toxic, and that alone should have killed me." [12]

- Although nationally recognized physician, gynecologist, and surgeon Dr. Richard Eby went to heaven and spent two minutes in hell, he could never forget the smell of Satan's domain as he was "being taken to the lowest bowels of the earth." In his book *Caught Up Into Paradise*, the doctor described the smell

as "horrid, nasty, stale, fetid, rotten and evil…
mixed together and concentrated."[13]

- When former US Army private Carl Knighton
  went on a drug binge and overdosed in the
  1990s, he said he "began going down and
  down and down" into "a deep pit" that was
  "pitch-black dark" and filled with a stench
  infinitely worse than anything he had ever
  smelled on earth.[14]

- Shortly after former atheist Matthew Botsford
  was shot and killed in March 1992 by an
  attacker, he found himself being tortured in
  a deep, pitch-black abyss by mocking demons
  while his skin was repeatedly burned off with
  flowing lava. "My flesh was re-formed [to be
  burned all over again]," Botsford said, "and
  there was this continual mocking, this sense
  of hopelessness, and evil in all sides. There was
  nothing good there. It was totally void."[15]

- Matthew Dovel attempted suicide as a young
  man, hoping to experience heaven but instead
  found himself "in mid-free fall into a pit that
  [was] pitch-black." Once in hell Dovel experienced levels of pain he never knew possible. [16]

- After Curtis "Earthquake" Kelley mixed
  cocaine with several other powerful drugs, his
  overdose opened his eyes to the spiritual realm,
  and he experienced hours of demonic torture.

In his book *Bound to Lose Destined to Win*, Kelley recounted lying in the backseat of a car and being taken into hell by demonic spirits:

> They snatched me out of my body and pulled me through the floor of the car. I saw the drive shaft underneath the car; then the spirits pulled me into the earth. As I traveled through the earth, I saw sewer pipes, rocks, and everything else that was inside the earth. I was dragged to a place in the earth that was red and black. Then the spirits dropped me to the bottom of a floor....

> The spirits laughed, grabbed me, and tormented me all over again. They beat me in the head with some kind of sledgehammer. Hideous and deformed demonic spirits of every size imaginable had a hold on me, and they did to me whatever they wanted. The torment was nonstop. I had no defense against them, and there was no place to run or hide.[17]

Even some well-known believers from generations past have told similar accounts of the underworld. In the sixteenth century Saint Teresa of Avila had a dramatic experience in which she was suddenly "plunged into hell." In her writings she described the same darkness, foul odors, and "unendurable" sufferings of every sort as in the previous accounts. It was the anguish of her soul, however, that brought the most pain: "If I said that the soul is continually being torn from the body, it would be nothing, for that implies the destruction of life by the hands of another; but here it is the soul itself that is tearing itself in pieces. I cannot describe that inward fire or that despair, surpassing all torments and all pain."[18]

Each of these believers experienced the anguish of hell and returned forever changed. In fact, most were so shaken they made radical changes in their lifestyles and committed to sharing their accounts for the rest of their lives, not to draw attention to themselves but to draw souls away from the very real hell they experienced. They are living proof that hell indeed is no fairy tale but instead the eternal destination of those who fail to surrender their lives to Jesus.

## THE AGONY OF HELL

Moses, David, Isaiah, Ezekiel, Jeremiah, and Yeshua all gave detailed descriptions of hell, all of which reiterated not only its reality but also the horror of that reality. Those living today who claim to have experienced hell in person confirm these horrors. The unquenchable thirst. The searing heat. The nakedness and vulnerability. The physical pain. The despair and regret of not acknowledging Jesus for who He is. The demonic torture. The void of communication, fellowship, and companionship—all replaced by the tormenting isolation.

In his account of the horrors of hell, Bill Wiese offers a description of what may be its most agonizing aspect:

> To experience the feeling of being lost forever was by far the worst part of hell. On earth, we always have some form of hope. Even amidst the most direful situations, we have hope that we'll escape, even if it's only through death. But there you know positively there is no hope whatsoever; you will never get out.

> Your soul cannot die, and you are lost and in tor-
> ment forever.[19]

It is difficult, if not impossible, for those of us on earth
to imagine the degree of hopelessness found in hell. During
Wiese's time there, he had no awareness of God, even though
he had been a believer for most of his life. It is this vacuum,
this utter void of the light and hope of God Himself, that
will be the despair of countless souls cast into the pit alongside the very father of that despair, Satan.

Hell was originally made for Satan and the other fallen
angels who rebelled against God (Matt. 25:41; 2 Pet. 2:4).
Because of this, most people think of hell as where Satan
currently lives. Even comic book portrayals of Lucifer routinely picture him with a pitchfork in his hand, standing
in a cavernous abode of flames with a sign reading "Hell"
hanging overhead. But the truth is that Satan is not confined
to hell right now. Jesus spoke of the devil as the "prince of
this world" (John 14:30, NIV), while Paul called him the "ruler
of the kingdom of the air" (Eph. 2:2, NIV). Both descriptions clearly indicate that Satan dwells on earth and is not
bound to hell. And in the Book of Revelation, Jesus said to
the church in Pergamum, "I know...where you live, where
Satan's throne is" (Rev. 2:13), and to the church in Smyrna,
"The devil is about to throw some of you into prison" (v. 10).

Satan's domain will change when the Messiah returns.
Revelation details that the devil will actually be bound
to hell and unable to dwell on earth anymore during the
thousand-year reign of Jesus:

> And I saw an angel coming down out of heaven,
> having the key to the bottomless pit and a great chain

in his hand. He seized the dragon, that ancient serpent, who is the Devil and Satan, and bound him for a thousand years. He cast him into the bottomless pit, and shut him up, and set a seal on him, that he should deceive the nations no more, until the thousand years were ended.

—REVELATION 20:1–3

As we have already discovered, "the bottomless pit" John referred to is hell itself. And what he said will happen when Satan is bound, locked up, and sealed in hell is hugely significant: the devil will "deceive the nations no more" (v. 3). For the first time in human history Satan will no longer be allowed to delude people. Although the devil was defeated when Jesus died on the cross and arose three days later, the Lord has still allowed Satan some room to roam the earth and cause destruction through his deceptive schemes. Jesus' return will mark the time when "that ancient serpent" will finally be confined. Yes!

The Hebrew Scriptures confirm the Book of Revelation's sequence of events. For example, the prophet Isaiah wrote:

In that day the LORD shall punish the host of heaven on high and the kings of the earth on the earth. They shall be gathered together, as prisoners are gathered in the dungeon, and shall be shut up in the prison, and after many days they shall be punished.

—ISAIAH 24:21–22

Notice how Isaiah pointed out that not only will Satan be punished but also all those who oppose God—both the spiritual "host" and earthly "kings." Together they will be shut up in what we have now seen described as a dungeon, prison, and bottomless pit. Again, this is clearly hell.

The "many days" Isaiah referred to in verse 22 are simply what John repeatedly described as the "thousand years" when Satan is bound (Rev. 20:2–7). In fact, John mentions this specific length of time six times in six verses! Why did he stress this *thousand-year* term so much? I believe it is because the Lord wanted us to know there is a definitive beginning and end to this period of peace on earth. Like the buildup to a movie's climactic showdown between the hero and villain, the millennial kingdom will end with one final attempt by Satan to overthrow the Lord.

## GOING OUT IN A BLAZE OF MISERY

John was specific in mentioning—and reiterating—how long Jesus would initially rule on earth without the presence of evil. Unfortunately for us, he was not so specific in describing what happens immediately after that when Satan is "set free for a little while" (Rev. 20:3). In fact, he spent only three verses giving us information for what may well be the most climactic battle ever:

> When the thousand years are ended, Satan will be set free from his prison and will go out to deceive the nations which are in the four corners of the earth, Gog and Magog, to gather them for battle. Their number is like the sand of the sea. They traveled the breadth of the earth and surrounded the camp of the saints and the beloved city. But fire came down from God out of heaven and devoured them.
>
> —REVELATION 20:7–9

Armageddon will be the ultimate world war, yet it will not be the final one, as most people think. There is still another battle, an even greater one since it will be Satan's last assault. After he is released, the devil will launch a rebellion to end all rebellions. He will spread as much deception throughout the earth as he can and once again try to take down as many of God's children as possible. Despite the global peace that will exist under Yeshua's reign, there will still be people born during His thousand-year government who do not come into a saving relationship with Yeshua. These are the ones whom Satan, upon his release, will "go out to deceive" (v. 8).

Despite the magnitude of this conflict, Scripture gives us only a bare-bones outline of these events (for reasons we will only know when we reach heaven). The outcome of this ultimate war will be the same as Armageddon, however: The Lord will win with little more than a thought and a command (sending fire from heaven to devour them), and Satan will once again lose, only this time he will be cast not into hell but into his final destination—the lake of fire.

> The devil, who deceived them, was cast into the lake of fire and brimstone where the beast and the false prophet were. They will be tormented day and night forever and ever.
>
> —REVELATION 20:10

## MOCKING HELL

Clearly hell is no laughing matter. Today many people joke about enjoying the sinful pleasures of life while they are knowingly and willingly on the "highway to hell." They mock hell's horrors by claiming that if hell is real, then it must be more fun than heaven, given how much they enjoy what God says is sin. And they say they want to go there because all their friends will be there too.

Sin has its consequences, however. Satan will not relent in his pursuit to "steal and kill and destroy" as many lives as he can (John 10:10). If misery loves company, then the devil surely desires the company of billions upon billions of souls in hell. He likes nothing better than to keep people believing that hell is a myth and, for those who actually believe in it, that it is not as bad as it sounds.

Beloved, hell is worse than bad. It is so bad Jesus said more than once that it would be better to cut off the parts of your body that cause you to go to hell than to end up in the place prepared for Satan. (See Matthew 5:29–30; 18:8–9; Mark 9:43–48.) Yeshua was fully aware that the masses would claim to enjoy the road to hell while being blind to its true horrors. This is why He told His followers in Matthew 7:13–14, "Enter by the narrow gate; for wide is the gate and broad is the way that leads to destruction, and there are many who go in by it. Because narrow is the gate and difficult is the way which leads to life, and there are few who find it" (NKJV).

Because Jesus warned us that sin would increase as the end times near, we can be certain that this narrow gate will seem even narrower in the coming days (Matt. 24:12). Our culture's disbelief in hell itself will continue to rise, as will the number of those who mock hell with their hedonistic lifestyles. It will be more difficult for believers to stand up in public and preach a gospel that includes hell. They will be persecuted for such "foolish" belief. But neither public opinion nor persecution changes the truth of hell. It is as real as the life you and I now live.

For those now awakening to the reality of hell, there is still time. We live in a season covered by God's grace and mercy, and because of this, those who cry out to Him for forgiveness and ask Him to be Lord of their lives will find a God who is quick to welcome them into His eternal kingdom. Many people come to the Lord by having a revelation of hell, and if you at this moment sense a need to be rescued, I encourage you to cry out to God right now.

If you know the Lord but after reading this chapter feel compelled by the Spirit to warn those around you of the reality of hell, know that now is the time to do so. Maybe loved ones in your family have yet to be saved, or maybe close friends or neighbors still do not know about God's love. Don't hesitate; *now* is the time for you to share the gospel! Hell and the lake of fire are real, but we can throw a rescue line to those destined for such misery. God "does not want any to perish, but all to come to repentance" (2 Pet. 3:9). His desire is to rescue those on their way to hell, but He has commissioned His people to be part of His rescue efforts. May we be bold enough to tell people about hell and, more importantly, about the God who loves them and wants to save them from such incomprehensible horror.

# CHAPTER 12

# THE MILLENNIAL REIGN OF THE MESSIAH

WHEN I WAS a young believer, I had a hard time reconciling the Jesus I saw in the Gospels with the Jesus I saw in the Book of Revelation. This was part of the reason I did not want to read Revelation. I, like so many believers, mistakenly saw two different versions of the Lord. The Gospel version included a Jesus who seemed soft, gentle, and kind, who healed the sick and gathered the children around Himself, and who talked about peace and love. I liked this Jesus. On the other hand, there was the Jesus in Revelation who came back to earth wearing a bloodied robe with a sword in His mouth and who commanded birds to feast on the flesh of His enemies. To be honest, Jesus seemed like a different person in Revelation than He did elsewhere in the Bible. This puzzled and scared me, so I stayed away from reading Revelation.

I am not alone in my experience. Countless believers have a hard time embracing John's vision, much less how he describes Jesus. They prefer to skip the tough passages of Jesus destroying the nations at Armageddon or sentencing people to hell at His judgment seat, and instead they fast-forward to the more enjoyable parts of the story—such as when we get to be with Him in heaven, reign with Him for a thousand years, and bask in His glory for eternity.

I empathize with people who may be confused by the Jesus we see in Revelation, as I have experienced a similar feeling.

But the longer I walk with Jesus, the more I discover that He is the same Lord in Revelation as He is in the Gospels. There is no disparity; He is the same loving yet powerful Messiah. The Jesus who showed His extreme love by dying on a cross for you and me is the same passionate Jesus who will return as the most powerful King of kings, with all authority to rule the earth and cleanse it from all unrighteousness.

Jesus knew people would struggle with the Book of Revelation. He knew people would doubt the reality of this apocalyptic vision and disregard many of its elements as either fairy tale or allegory. For this reason the Holy Spirit specifically inspired John to conclude his account by saying:

> I testify to everyone who hears the words of the prophecy of this book: If anyone adds to these things, God shall add to him the plagues that are written in this book. And if anyone takes away from the words of the book of this prophecy, God shall take away his part out of the Book of Life and out of the Holy City and out of the things which are written in this book.
>
> —REVELATION 22:18–19

Wow! What kind of a "Don't touch" sign is that? Yet John's severe warning is there for a reason. Jesus was fully aware that this book would become the most misunderstood in the entire Bible. Revelation can seem overwhelming and even confusing upon first take. It contains many extraordinary—dare I say strange—parts and is certainly not presented in a neat, orderly, linear timeline. But none of those things changes its importance or its validity; in fact, it is one of the most important books in the New Testament.

The Book of Revelation is not a figurative allegory of God's plan for the world but a very real account of what will happen in the last days. Sure, some verses may be interpreted in different ways, and some may lean heavily on symbolic language. But its portrayal of Jesus is accurate, and its events are real.

I hope our journey has proved not only that Revelation can be understood but also that it must be understood through the lens of the Hebrew prophets, who had much to say about the same events and circumstances that John described. Before we move on to one of the greatest of these events, the thousand-year reign of Messiah, let's quickly review the sequence of latter events surrounding Jesus' return so we can better understand the context of His establishing a new kingdom on earth.

When the seventh and last trumpet of God's judgment sounds, the dead who have been redeemed by the Lamb will rise and meet the Lord in the air, along with the raptured believers living during the tribulation. This will mark the long-awaited marriage union between Yeshua and His bride, the church, and will kick off the greatest celebration ever, the "marriage supper of the Lamb." While believers experience heights of ecstasy and joy we cannot imagine, those in the world will experience the anguish of God's wrath poured out in all its fullness. Once the seven bowls of His wrath have been emptied, Jesus will then return to earth.

When He returns, the Lord will save the entire nation of Israel, utterly destroy His enemies, and rid the planet of all wickedness. With His authority now unquestioned, Jesus will sit in the judgment seat and, much to the delight of those who serve Him, reward believers for their deeds on earth. Yet in this same seat He also will judge the sin of the unredeemed and send them, along with Satan and all those who sided against Him, to the bottomless pit of hell for a thousand years. This will mark the beginning of the millennial reign of Yeshua HaMashiach, who will lead the greatest kingdom the earth will ever know.

## CHANGE IN LEADERSHIP

One of the most obvious and significant reasons we long for Jesus to return and establish His kingdom is that it will mark the end of evil reigning upon the earth. The Bible says that during this present age, "The whole world is under the control of the evil one," who is Satan (1 John 5:19, NIV). When Jesus returns and begins to rule, the devil's dominion will finally fall.

We can hardly imagine what a world *not* under Satan's authority is like, given that since the fall our planet has been exponentially saturated with humanity's sin and Satan's rule. None of us has ever experienced an existence devoid of evil's influence. But during the Messiah's millennial reign the devil and all the forces of destruction, sickness, depression, violence, and evil will be bound. John depicts this in the first verses of Revelation 20, which we read in the previous chapter but which I will highlight again:

And I saw an angel coming down out of heaven, having the key to the bottomless pit and a great chain in his hand. He seized the dragon, that ancient serpent, who is the Devil and Satan, and bound him for a thousand years. He cast him into the bottomless pit, and shut him up, and set a seal on him, that he should deceive the nations no more, until the thousand years were ended.

—REVELATION 20:1–3

Mankind will experience a respite from evil and all its effects while Satan is imprisoned for a thousand years. Our planet will undergo a dramatic shift in leadership as authority is passed from the current "ruler of this world" (John 14:30; 2 Cor. 4:4), Satan, to the rightful "KING OF KINGS AND LORD OF LORDS," King Jesus (Rev. 19:16). Of course, ultimately all dominion and power rests with God, who has complete authority over everything and everyone—including Satan. But after the devil's defeat at Armageddon, Jesus will come before the Father and officially assume full reign of the earth as its rightful King. The prophet Daniel depicted this significant leadership transfer when Yeshua will come before Father God, whom Daniel called the "Ancient of Days":

I saw in the night visions, and there was one like a Son of Man [Yeshua] coming with the clouds of heaven. He came to the Ancient of Days [the Father] and was presented before Him. There was given to Him dominion, and glory, and a kingdom, that all peoples, nations, and languages should serve Him. His dominion is an everlasting dominion, which shall not pass away, and His kingdom that which shall not be destroyed.

—DANIEL 7:13–14

The Lord's kingdom is everlasting, and it will have no barriers or obstacles when His thousand-year rule on earth begins. We will soon dive into the descriptions found throughout the Old and New Testaments of what this undisturbed kingdom will look like. But before we do, notice first how the apostle John explains that we, as God's children, will play a vital part in it.

> I saw thrones, and they sat on them, and the authority to judge was given to them....They came to life and reigned with Christ for a thousand years....Blessed and holy is he who takes part...[for] they shall be priests of God and of Christ and shall reign with Him a thousand years.
> —Revelation 20:4, 6

Who is John talking about here? Us! The fact that we, mere humans, have the privilege of reigning with Jesus for a thousand years is nothing short of staggering. What kind of Creator allows His creation to rule alongside Him? Only our God! He is a generous God, the giver of "every good gift and every perfect gift" who delights in sharing His glory (Jas. 1:17). Rather than reign alone, Yeshua has chosen to reign with and through us. He calls us priests and will give us heavenly thrones, bestow upon us authority, and invite us to govern this new earthly kingdom with Him. How amazing!

This invitation seems even more remarkable when we realize it was described throughout the Tanakh. Psalm 2 prophesies how the Father will turn over the world to the Messiah, marking the beginning of His millennial reign. In this rich Messianic psalm the Father tells Yeshua, "Ask of Me, and I will give you the nations for your inheritance, and the ends of the earth for your possession" (v. 8). Jesus has every right, as given by the Father, to rule the world alone, yet He has chosen to share that privilege with us! After He takes full possession of earth, the Lord will share His authority with His bride and make us co-laborers with Him. He has pledged, "To him who overcomes and keeps My works to the end, I will give authority over the nations" (Rev. 2:26). In Matthew 5:5 Jesus promised that the meek will be blessed, "for they shall inherit the earth." And as we saw in chapter 10, He will entrust more to those who have been more faithful to Him on earth in the present time.

## LIFE IN THE KINGDOM

We know we will rule and reign with Jesus because of His extraordinary invitation to us. But what will life actually be like during the millennium? What will things look like on earth when Jesus is in full control? To answer this, we need simply to remind ourselves of the core of Jesus' model prayer, what we call the Lord's Prayer.

When Yeshua was teaching His disciples to pray, the first statement He made after addressing the Father was, "Your kingdom come; Your will be done on earth, as it is in heaven" (Matt. 6:10). The church's mission on earth is to bring about and expand God's kingdom "on earth, as it is in heaven." Likewise, when Jesus' kingdom is fully established on earth, we can safely predict that "on earth" it will be "as it is in heaven."

At last the earth will match up with heaven, as it did when God first created it. That means there will be no sorrow, sickness, suffering, or pain. Peace and beauty will exist in every corner of the world. In fact, the physical landscape will be different because nature will be completely restored and no longer permeated with the elements of death or decay. All of creation will adhere to the Lord's ruling spirit of peace, just as Isaiah prophesied more than twenty-seven hundred years ago in one of Scripture's most detailed portraits of the millennial landscape:

> The wolf also shall dwell with the lamb, and the leopard shall lie down with the young goat, and the calf and the young lion and the fatling together.... The cow and the bear shall graze; their young ones shall lie down together; and the lion shall eat straw like the ox. The nursing child shall play by the hole of the asp, and the weaned child shall put his hand in the viper's den. They shall not hurt or destroy in all My holy mountain, for the earth shall be full of the knowledge of the LORD, as the waters cover the sea.
>
> —ISAIAH 11:6–9

Creatures that once lived as enemies in violent pursuit or fear of each other will suddenly dwell side by side in complete harmony. All creation will exist in peace with one another because we all will be fully submitted to the Prince of Peace, Jesus Christ. Isaiah continued his vivid description of Yeshua's millennial kingdom later in his prophetic book:

> The voice of weeping shall no longer be heard in [the land], nor the voice of crying. There shall no longer be an infant who lives only a few days nor an old man who has not filled out his days....They shall not labor in vain nor bring forth children for trouble; for they are the descendants of the blessed of the LORD and their offspring with them....The wolf and the

> lamb shall feed together, and the lion shall eat straw
> like the bull.
>
> —ISAIAH 65:19–20, 23, 25

If this sounds like heaven on earth, that is because it will be. And if it sounds like the Garden of Eden before mankind fell, that is because once again it will be. Jesus' second coming will cleanse the earth of its evil and sin, and His millennial kingdom will restore it to its perfect original state. As Paul said, the Father will "unite all things in Christ, which are in heaven and on earth" (Eph. 1:10).

One of the greatest aspects of the garden was not just the perfect creation surrounding Adam and Eve but also the perfect union between them and the Lord. Adam and Eve shared a pure intimacy with the Lord that allowed them to walk naked and unashamed before Him—such was the degree of their union. This was not a sexual intimacy. It was instead the deepest intimacy shared on every possible level— the intimacy for which God created us.

The millennial kingdom will reintroduce humanity to a closeness with God so profound and fulfilling that nothing we have experienced up to this point in life comes close to it. Remember, we were created in our maker's image to have relationship with Him. When Jesus raptures the church and we are finally united with Him in the marriage supper of the Lamb, our relationship will be restored to an intimacy that surpasses even what Adam and Eve had before the fall. We will walk in the fullness of our purpose. We will be married to Jesus; He will be our husband, and we will be His bride.

Although my wife and I are two completely different people, we still commune with a supernatural oneness.

Sometimes the Holy Spirit will allow us to feel what the other one is going through even if we are geographically separated from each other. At other times the Lord will allow me to suddenly feel Cynthia's heart right in the middle of an argument we are having, which will completely correct my attitude. I so appreciate these sudden divine interruptions because not only do they take me to such a different dimension than the stress we're dealing with on the surface, but they also allow me to change my perspective. When I am able to truly "feel" my wife's emotions and become conscious of her heart, immediately everything changes, and I can love her the way that I should.

The intimacy husbands and wives can experience with each other is truly divine. Yet our marital unions are but a drop in the bucket compared with what all believers will experience with the Lord in the millennial kingdom. If I can at times finish my wife's sentences or guess her thoughts without her saying a word, can you imagine what God can do? "Before they call, I will answer; and while they are yet speaking, I will hear," the Lord said in Isaiah's prophecy about the kingdom to come (Isa. 65:24). The intimacy we share with Him in a world restored and ruled by Jesus will be unlike anything we can presently fathom!

## RULING WITH RIGHTEOUSNESS

Throughout history many leaders have tried to bring peace on earth. The goal of establishing utopia is nothing new. A delusional Adolf Hitler thought he could bring utopia by populating the world with a "superior" Aryan race of people. Abraham Lincoln assumed he could bring utopia by freeing slaves. Alexander the Great thought he could gain it by conquering lands. Winston Churchill. Joseph Stalin. Thomas Jefferson. Fidel Castro. Saddam Hussein. Idi Amin. John Fitzgerald Kennedy. Benito Mussolini. Mao Tse-tung. Vladimir Lenin. All these leaders thought they could bring peace on earth. Some went about that in peaceful ways, while others abused their power in an attempt to fulfill their goal. All certainly had different ideas of what "peace on earth" looked like. And ultimately all failed.

Only one person in all of history will succeed at bringing lasting peace upon the earth, and His name is Jesus. Yeshua HaMashiach will establish true utopia! We again turn to the prophet Isaiah for some of the details:

> The Spirit of the LORD shall rest upon him, the Spirit of wisdom and understanding, the Spirit of counsel and might, the Spirit of knowledge and of the fear of the LORD. He shall delight in the fear of the LORD, and he shall not judge by what his eyes see, nor reprove by what his ears hear; but *with righteousness he shall judge the poor, and reprove with fairness for the meek of the earth....Righteousness shall be the belt of his loins*, and faithfulness the belt about his waist....In that day there shall be a Root of Jesse, who shall stand as a banner to the peoples. For him shall the nations seek. And his rest shall be glorious.
>
> —ISAIAH 11:2–5, 10, EMPHASIS ADDED

Jesus will rule with righteousness, which means every decision, motive, judgment, and action He makes will stem from His perfect character. It is easy to trust a leader when you know he or she will always be fair, kind, just, loving, and humble. Jesus will far surpass the world's most honorable leaders because He is every perfect attribute blended into one perfect person. As a result, the world will love Him and love being under His leadership. As Proverbs 29:2 says, "When the righteous are in authority, the people rejoice." It will be sheer joy to be a citizen of Yeshua's kingdom on earth because He will cause justice and righteousness to saturate the land, just as the ancient Hebrew prophets foretold:

> The days are coming, says the LORD, that I will raise up for David a righteous Branch [the Messiah], and he shall reign as king and deal wisely, and shall execute justice and righteousness in the earth. In his days Judah will be saved, and Israel will dwell safely. And this is the name by which he will be called: THE LORD OUR RIGHTEOUSNESS.
>
> —JEREMIAH 23:5–6

When complete justice and righteousness flow from every aspect of government, not only will Israel "dwell safely," but also the whole world will. There will be no need to fear an attack from a neighboring country or the neighbor down the street. We will no longer have to lock our doors at night or keep an eye on our children at all times, and this is how it will be throughout the millennium. With the absence of evil, fear will have no presence in Jesus' kingdom.

All of us know what it is like to be tormented by fear. Fears come in many shapes, colors, and sizes. While one person is afraid of growing old, another fears losing money. One may be afraid of getting robbed or raped, while another fears failure. The list of what we fear goes on and on. The reality is, Satan uses fear as his greatest weapon to torment those of us whom God loves.

I remember a time in my life when Satan kept me in dread of something concerning my two daughters, both of whom were young at the time. I would go to sleep each night praying for them as a way to respond to the fear. I remember looking in the bathroom mirror each night as I brushed my teeth, struggling with thoughts of fear concerning their safety and well-being. Night after night it was the same. It truly was tormenting. But eventually the Lord taught me how to use His Word against those fears, and He brought a good degree of deliverance to me in this area.

All of us have been tormented by fear—it's a constant force in the world today. But when Yeshua reigns, fear will have been vanquished, and we will truly live in spiritual peace that will cover the earth. Because of our righteous ruler, everyone will be blessed!

## CHANNEL OF BLESSING

We can hardly imagine a world filled with such righteousness and peace. Indeed the Lord will cover the earth with His blessings. Yet just as He has always done, He will use a familiar channel to release this blessing: His chosen people, Israel.

Think about it: This will be the only time in history when all Israel will be walking rightly with Him. This will unlock worldwide blessing for all during the millennial kingdom.

As we have observed throughout this book, God purposed from the days of Abraham that Israel would be the channel through which He would bless the entire earth. So when every Jewish person on the planet calls upon the name of Jesus, can you imagine the blessings that will pour out to the rest of the nations? Paul said if the world was blessed when Israel rejected the gospel—because by rejecting it, the gospel came to the Gentiles—what will it be like when Israel receives the good news of Yeshua HaMashiach (Rom. 11:12)? The apostle answered that question by saying it will be like "life from the dead" for God's people (Rom. 11:15).

Remember, Jesus was Jewish. The last description He gave of Himself in the Bible was a reminder of His Jewish heritage. In Revelation 22:16 He said, "I am the Root and the Offspring of David." So when He returns and establishes His millennial kingdom, I highly doubt His eternal connection to Israel will suddenly become inconsequential or be disregarded. Instead Jesus will bring divine alignment to the world *through* His chosen people. When Israel is blessed, the whole world benefits, and this timeless principle will continue into the millennial kingdom, where Yeshua will bless the nations through His chosen people.

Zechariah 8:23 relays what life will be like in a time of such blessing: "In those days ten men from every language of the nations will take hold of the garment of a Jew, saying, 'Let us go with you, for we have heard that God is with you.'" The Lord's blessing will be upon the Jewish people, and this will bring unimaginable prosperity.

Because of this covenant of blessing with Israel, it is not difficult to guess where Yeshua will establish the centerpiece of His rule on earth during His thousand-year reign. Just as every kingdom has a capital where the heart of that nation's government lies, so the Lord will set up the centerpiece of His authority from Israel's central city, Jerusalem. The prophet Zechariah prophesied its rebuilding for the millennial kingdom more than twenty-five hundred years ago:

> Thus says the LORD of Hosts: I have a great jeal-
> ousy for Jerusalem and Zion....I have returned to
> Jerusalem with mercy, and My house will be built in
> it, says the LORD of Hosts, and a measuring line will
> be stretched over Jerusalem....Yet again My cities
> will overflow with goodness, and again the LORD
> will comfort Zion and choose Jerusalem.
>
> —ZECHARIAH 1:14, 16–17

Zechariah goes on to explain that after Armageddon, Jerusalem shall be "raised up" (Zech. 14:10, NIV) and everything in it made "holy" (vv. 20–21).

Jerusalem is the spiritual center of the world. In fact, when a Jewish person goes to Jerusalem from any part of the earth, he is said to be making aliyah, which is the Hebrew word meaning to go up or to ascend.[1] Just as God revealed to me in my vision that Israel is elevated high above the earth, Jerusalem is the world's spiritual summit. Though the city is currently divided, the Lord promised in the passage we just read that He will build His house again in Jerusalem. In fact, in Ezekiel 40–48 we find an incredibly detailed account of what the new temple will be like there. God is jealous for Jerusalem and is longing for the day when it will serve as the administrative center of His kingdom. "Out of Zion, the perfection of beauty, God has shined," the psalmist prophesied in Psalm 50:2. Indeed the light of the Lord will emanate out of the highest spiritual point, Jerusalem, and flood the world with its truth, righteousness, justice, peace, and love.

This scene—of divine government resting "on earth, as it is in heaven"—will fulfill one of Isaiah's first prophecies:

In the last days, the mountain of the LORD's house
shall be established on the top of the mountains, and
shall be exalted above the hills, and all nations shall
flow to it. Many people shall go and say, "Come, and
let us go up to the mountain of the LORD, to the
house of the God of Jacob, and He will teach us of
His ways, and we will walk in His paths." For out
of Zion shall go forth the law, and the word of the
LORD from Jerusalem.

—ISAIAH 2:2–3

As the righteous government of the Lord pours out of
Jerusalem, yet another prophecy from the Tanakh will
become reality: "The earth will be filled with the knowledge of the glory of the LORD, as the waters cover the seas"
(Hab. 2:14). This is why we are commanded to "pray for the
peace of Jerusalem" (Ps. 122:6). Understand, there will not
really be peace in Jerusalem until the Messiah returns. Did
you know that Jerusalem, or Yerushalayim in Hebrew, literally means "city of peace"? As has been mentioned, countless world leaders have tried to establish utopia, and some of
them even tried to establish it in Jerusalem. This is impossible, however, because the only way peace will rule in
Jerusalem is through divine intervention. So when we pray
for the peace of Jerusalem, what we are really praying for is
for Yeshua HaMashiach to return to set up His kingdom on
earth and to reign from Jerusalem. The Prince of Peace will
govern from this city of peace, bringing peace on earth, even
"as the waters cover the seas" (Hab. 2:14).

## CALLING FOR HIS COMING

Again, when we pray for the peace of Jerusalem, we are calling for Jesus to come. As we call out to God, He responds. There is not a single word spoken on this earth that God cannot hear, nor is there a whispered prayer He does not pay attention to. When Hagar, Sarah's servant, found herself alone in the desert and called out to the Lord, He showed Himself true as the God who hears (Gen. 16:11). When Elijah called upon the Lord to send rain after three and a half years of drought, God heard his persistent cries and answered (1 Kings 18:41–45). First John 5:14 promises that we can be confident "that if we ask anything according to His will, He hears us."

Remember, Yeshua *wants* to return to earth. It is His will to see sin and evil expelled from our planet and to bring about His kingdom of righteousness. Yet the timing of His coming is connected to two things.

First, Jesus' coming is connected to our calling for Him to come. This is why our prayers asking Him to come *really* matter. It is also why John's last declaration in the Book of Revelation is, "Even so, come Lord Jesus!" (Rev. 22:20).

When we pray for Jesus to come—for Him to return to earth—we are most definitely praying "according to His will." That means He hears us and will respond! John exhorts the church to call on Jesus when he says, "The Spirit and the bride say, 'Come.' Let him who hears say, 'Come'" (Rev. 22:17).

Why, then, has Yeshua not already responded? Because of the second element tied to His coming: our condition. Second Peter 3:9 clearly addresses this when it says: "The Lord is not slow concerning His promise, as some count slowness. But He is patient with us, because He does not want any to perish, but all to come to repentance." The Lord is waiting for all those He has chosen to come to Him and for His church to repent and turn to Him.

Jesus is waiting for a bride prepared to be joined with Him, and a people ready to rule and reign with Him. As the great husband, He wants to hear that His wife (the church) desires to be with Him, as any husband would want—thus the importance of our calling to Him. But as the great King, He also needs a people who are *able* to rule with Him.

I believe the Lord will use persecution to make us ready. In Daniel 12 the prophet seemed to suggest the same thing when he said that during "a time of trouble such as never was" (v. 1), which clearly is the end times, "many shall be purified and made white and tried" (v. 10). Daniel also indicated that the church will be persecuted by the Antichrist (Dan. 7:25), but that in the end "all the kingdoms under the whole heaven...shall be given to the people of the saints of the Most High" (v. 27).

Those who endure persecution and are purified through it will possess the kingdom and rule with Yeshua in the millennium (Dan. 7:22). Jesus even promised this to His twelve disciples during His ministry on earth when He said, "When the Son of Man sits on His glorious throne, you who have followed Me will also sit on twelve thrones, judging the twelve tribes of Israel" (Matt. 19:28).

But Yeshua did not communicate this or any of the other scriptures we have looked at in this chapter merely to get us excited about the millennial kingdom or to get our theology right about His rule. He shared these things with us so we can change our lives *now*!

## PREPARING TO INVEST

Jesus desires for each of us to be ready to rule with Him. We must take whatever actions are necessary for us to prepare for His second coming. That includes growing and maximizing the gifts, talents, time, and resources God has given us.

God is an investor. In fact, His investing strategy is far greater than that of Warren Buffett or any Wall Street hotshot. God has invested in us the very seeds of His kingdom, but He expects those seeds to produce fruit so His kingdom can expand "on earth, as it is in heaven" (Matt. 6:10). Jesus told a parable in the Gospel of Luke that explains this expectation further:

> A nobleman went to a distant country to receive a kingdom for himself, and then return. And he called ten of his slaves, and gave them ten minas and said to them, 'Do business with this until I come back.' But his citizens hated him and sent a delegation after him, saying, 'We do not want this man to reign over us.' When he returned, after receiving the kingdom, he ordered that these slaves, to whom he had given the money, be called to him so that he might know what business they had done.
>
> —LUKE 19:12–15, NASB

A mina was equal to a hundred days' wages, so ten minas was almost three years' salary. This was no small amount. As anyone would, the nobleman expected his servants to grow the business by earning a return on his money. As the story continues, the nobleman finds that each of the first two servants he calls have invested wisely and gained 100 and

50 percent returns, respectively. Their reward is to each rule over the same number of cities they have earned individually. Wow—talk about a massive reward! These men go from slaves to princes, inheriting entire cities just for being good stewards with their master's resources.

Another servant comes to report to the nobleman and, having hid his portion instead of investing it, offers an excuse: He was afraid. Unlike his coworkers, this servant receives nothing. In fact, the nobleman harshly rebukes him, takes away his portion, and gives it to someone else.

Beloved, God has entrusted to each of us resources to be used for Him while we are on this earth. These come in many forms: our talents, gifts, time, money, energy, ideas— the list goes on. The ultimate purpose for those gifts is not to grow our personal kingdoms, improve our worldly portfolio, or even bury the gifts in the sand. We are to build His kingdom. In Hebrew we call this *tikkun olam*, meaning that God has given us the responsibility to heal the world and bring reconciliation to it. In short, we are to bring about the kingdom of God "on earth, as it is in heaven." Yeshua brought the kingdom of God to earth. Just as the nobleman did in the parable, Jesus has called us to expand this kingdom in whatever sphere we live as we "do business."

Doing kingdom business is not easy, however. We will face opposition and plenty of "haters." Much of the world today hates the idea that one day God will have the last say. Like the citizens in the parable, they "do not want this man to reign" over them (Luke 19:14). They want to throw out God's standards in every area of life. Indeed in America they have thrown out the Ten Commandments. They have thrown out teaching about creation. They have thrown out prayer in public and any symbols of our faith in God. And this trend is intensifying.

But despite the increasing opposition to God's rule and His standards, our task remains the same: We are to engage in kingdom pursuits to build His kingdom—to make *tikkun olam* on the earth, and to be salt and light in the world. Jesus said, "To him who overcomes and keeps My works to the end, I will give authority over the nations" (Rev. 2:26). The more we grow His kingdom now, the more we prove that we can rule with Him in His millennial kingdom to come. And if we remain true to our assignment, we will reign with Him. We also are promised an even greater reward, however. As we call for Him to return, we are promised Jesus Himself.

CHAPTER 13

# THE NEW HEAVEN AND THE NEW EARTH

IN THE 1997 movie *Contact,* Jodie Foster's character, scientist Eleanor "Ellie" Arroway, seems to take a journey through space and time to make contact with extraterrestrial beings. With the whole world on the edge of its seat listening to Ellie's account, she does her best to describe every second and every sight as any scientist would traveling at light speed through wormholes, galaxies, and uncharted space. Yet in one of the movie's most poignant scenes there is a moment when her spaceship suddenly stops its journey and floats in space. As she turns her attention away from her ship and toward the heavens, her words instantly cease as well.

She is stunned. Awestruck. Overwhelmed. Tears begin to flow as pure amazement overcomes her. "No...no words," she eventually whispers. "No words to describe. Poetry. They should've sent a poet—it's so beautiful. Beautiful. So beautiful. So beautiful..."[1]

Her words trail off as the camera zooms in, capturing the look of absolute wonder on her face. Despite all her years of study and research as a scientist, despite all her knowledge as the world's foremost expert in extraterrestrial intelligence, despite a lifetime spent preparing for this moment, Ellie is at a complete loss for words to describe what her eyes behold. "I...had...no...idea," she finally says. "I had no idea."[2]

Though this is a weak and totally inadequate example compared with the reality of what heaven will be like, it still illustrates the point: None of us can fully fathom what heaven will be like. Like Ellie, we will be mesmerized, stunned, and left in wonder-filled amazement when we enter into what the Bible calls heaven.

Most of us at some point have tried to imagine what heaven will be like. The truth is, it will be unlike anything we have ever imagined because it is not of this world, and what it is made of is not in this world. This is why John used the word *like* throughout the Book of Revelation when describing elements of heaven (Rev. 4:1, 3, 6–7; 6:1; 10:1, 3; 14:2, 14; 19:6, 12; 21:11). For example, when the apostle first saw Jesus sitting on His throne, John described Him as One who "appeared *like* a jasper and a sardius stone," while the sea before His throne was "*like* crystal" (Rev. 4:3, 6, emphasis added). Later John described a heavenly person (possibly Jesus) whose "face was *like* the sun, and his feet *like* pillars of fire" (Rev. 10:1, emphasis added). Simply put, there was nothing on earth with which he could actually compare these things. Even the earth's most beautiful, majestic, and awesome sights are but a glimpse of God's domain. The greatest, most fulfilling, most moving experiences in this world cannot match what awaits us in heaven.

Perhaps you can relate to a sense of trying to imagine heaven but feeling as if you are grasping at straws. Simply put, the idea of heaven overwhelms our human minds. We cannot fully understand the concept of eternity, much less an eternal place where God Himself dwells and that He wants to share with us. Because of our limited scope, we struggle to completely comprehend what God has in store for us in heaven. Paul said, "Eye has not seen, nor ear heard, nor has it entered into the heart of man the things which God has prepared for those who love Him" (1 Cor. 2:9).

Although the Bible confirms in verses like this that we are limited in our grasp of heaven, that does not mean God's Word is silent on the matter. In fact, as we conclude our look at the Book of Revelation, I am thankful that heaven is the final topic. John ends his book by describing a beautiful and glorious heavenly scene and by reminding us of our heavenly home-to-be. This is not a coincidence.

I believe we are each born with a sense of heaven and eternity in us, and this impression does not go away easily. (After all, we are made in God's image.) As a child I imagined a pseudo-heavenly paradise where I would float down a beautiful tropical river with emerald water and lush fruit trees on both sides. This heaven of my childhood also was filled with green plants and colorful, singing birds. Today I don't picture the same heaven, but I still long for eternity—for a place where I am surrounded by God's glory and His perfection rather than the broken, bent-toward-evil world that surrounds me. You probably long for this too. This world can hurt, disappoint, frustrate, and destroy. But the heaven we find in the Bible is the opposite. In fact, as we discover more about heaven in this chapter, we will see that we truly have no idea just how wonderful it is.

## A PHYSICAL HEAVEN

The Hebrew word for heaven, *sha'meh*, has many different variations, yet all relate to a place of heights that is lofty and elevated.[3] First Kings 8:30 indicates that it is God's "dwelling place" above, from where He hears our prayers. More than once Jesus spoke of ascending—going *up*—to heaven (John 3:13; 20:17), and numerous accounts of the ascension specifically tell of Jesus being "carried up into heaven"

(Luke 24:51; see also Mark 16:19; Acts 1:9–11). Throughout the Bible we find many such references to heaven being high above, up in the air, and beyond our world. But those are only generic phrases pointing us upward, not directions to an exact physical location. Because God exists outside of time and space as we know it, most people have concluded that heaven is a purely spiritual realm.

For all our uncertainty as to exactly where heaven is, however, Scripture is clear that it is not just a spiritual state but also has a physical element. This is a new concept for many people, including believers. For years I did not realize that heaven was an actual location, albeit not in an earthly sense. I thought that when I died I would simply be a spirit dwelling in Yahweh's presence in some spiritual plane of existence that we cannot comprehend while on earth. I imagined spending the rest of eternity as a spirit in the great glory of the Father, experiencing His awesome holiness.

Although that description is true, this is not all we have to look forward to in heaven. Those of us who believe in Yeshua as Lord and Savior have a physical place called heaven awaiting us, not just a state of existence or spiritual plane where we dwell in perpetual bliss with God's presence surrounding us. Heaven is an actual, literal, physical *place*. Jesus said, "In My Father's house are many dwelling places. If it were not so, I would have told you. I am going to prepare a place for you. And if I go and prepare a place for you, I will come again and receive you to Myself, that where I am, you may be also" (John 14:2–3).

It took me awhile to realize that heaven was an actual place. But as I began to study the Scriptures more, not only did I see this was true, but I also discovered something else just as shocking to me: The place where believers go when they die now is not the same heaven they will be in for eternity.

Confused? Then let's look at what the Bible says about this to better understand.

## FIRST HEAVEN

In Revelation 21:1 John wrote, "Then I saw 'a new heaven and a new earth.' For the first heaven and the first earth had passed away, and there was no more sea." This is a foundational scripture for recognizing that the Bible indeed distinguishes between a first heaven and a second, new heaven. We will soon delve into why and how John makes a distinction between the two, but for now I want us to recognize what the first heaven is.

Jesus alluded to this first heaven several times during His ministry, and shortly before He died He called it by a different name. While hanging on the cross, Yeshua promised the thief beside Him, "Today you will be with Me in Paradise" (Luke 23:43). As it was for the thief on the cross, paradise is the place believers go to when they die. John mentioned paradise early in the Book of Revelation (2:7) and then recorded a vision of this first heaven—which is the one that currently exists—in Revelation 4. His description is intense.

> There was a throne set in heaven with One sitting on the throne! ...There was a rainbow around the throne, appearing like an emerald. Twenty-four thrones were around the throne. And I saw twenty-four elders sitting on the thrones, clothed in white garments. They had crowns of gold on their heads. Lightnings and thunderings and voices proceeded

from the throne. Seven lamps of fire were burning
before the throne, which are the seven Spirits of
God. Before the throne was a sea of glass like crystal.
—REVELATION 4:2–6

If that was not intense enough for you, then try reading
the rest of Revelation 4, where John described creatures
around the throne with six wings, eyes covering their entire
bodies, and faces that look like a lion, calf, eagle, and man.
Definitely not of this world!

Although John's vision may sound strange, the important
thing to know about this heaven is its central focus: Jesus. The
four creatures are lost in worship and adoration of the Lord,
continually crying without end, "Holy, holy, holy is the Lord
God Almighty, who was, and is, and is to come" (Rev. 4:8, NIV).
As these creatures worship, the twenty-four elders cannot help
but join in. They cast their crowns before God's throne and
offer their praise: "You are worthy, O Lord, to receive glory
and honor and power; for You have created all things, and by
Your will they exist and were created" (Rev. 4:11).

As this magnificent scene in heaven continues, we find
millions upon millions of heavenly beings lending their
voices with the unprecedented worship:

Then I looked, and I heard around the throne and
the living creatures and the elders the voices of
many angels, numbering ten thousand times ten
thousand, and thousands of thousands, saying with
a loud voice: "Worthy is the Lamb who was slain, to
receive power and riches and wisdom and strength
and honor and glory and blessing!"
—REVELATION 5:11–12

Finally all creation—every living being in heaven and across the universe—is compelled to join in:

> Then I heard every creature which is in heaven and on the earth and under the earth and in the sea, and all that are in them, saying: "To Him who sits on the throne and to the Lamb be blessing and honor and glory and power, forever and ever!"
>
> —REVELATION 5:13

If you could combine all the world's greatest worship services into one, it still wouldn't scratch the surface of what worship before the King of kings will be like in heaven. We truly cannot comprehend how overwhelming and fulfilling it will be to stand before the Lord and worship Him alongside everything He has made. And this is only the beginning of what we have to look forward to when we get to the first heaven! There we also will be with all our family members and friends who were saved, as well as countless heroes of the faith throughout history and even martyrs who die during the end-time tribulation. (See Revelation 6:9–11.) What we experience in this heaven will dwarf all the greatest experiences we have ever had on earth. And because Jesus will have rewarded us at this point for the works we did on the earth, we will begin to enjoy these eternal rewards. It truly will be more than we can imagine.

## SECOND HEAVEN

It is hard to picture things getting any better than what I have described, and yet they will. Therein lies the "catch" of this first heaven: It will not last forever. As we have already seen, this is why John said, "Then I saw 'a new heaven and a new earth.' *For the first heaven and the first earth had passed away*, and there was no more sea" (Rev. 21:1, emphasis added). John intentionally pointed out the *passing away* of the first heaven to distinguish it from a second, future heaven—one that will be eternal.

Here is what I believe Scripture teaches: As the Messiah's millennial reign concludes, every person who has ever lived will gather at God's great white throne. After this judgment, hell will be thrown into the lake of fire. Then, according to John, there will be "a new heaven and a new earth" because "the first heaven and the first earth had passed away, and there was no more sea" (Rev. 21:1).

Why would John specifically point out that there was no more sea? Because in his vision of the heaven that currently exists (the first heaven) there was a sea. Earlier in the Book of Revelation he described this as "a sea of glass like crystal" before the throne of God in heaven (Rev. 4:6). John may have written Revelation when he was older, but don't think for a moment that his age affected his memory of this unforgettable vision; he was as sharp as ever! I believe John wanted us to note the difference between the two heavens he saw. More importantly, I believe he wanted us to know that as incredible as his throne room description was of the creatures, elders, angels, saints, and all creation worshipping in the heaven that now exists, it would be surpassed by "a new heaven and a new earth" (Rev. 21:1).

Twenty-seven hundred years earlier Isaiah had seen a similar vision. He prophesied that the Lord would "create new heavens and a new earth; the former things shall not be remembered or come to mind" (Isa. 65:17; 66:22). Why will we not remember things from the past once we reach this new heaven? Because the ecstasy we will experience in this eternal home with God will so dwarf our past experiences that they will not even come to mind! That is how much we will enjoy the new heaven.

I hope you can see how once again the Tanakh and B'rit Hadashah fit like a hand in a glove. Despite the mass of years between them, John and Isaiah both used the exact same wording to describe a "new heaven," and each gave unique information confirming that there is a difference between the first and second heavens.

## NEW EARTH, NEW BODIES

In addition to differentiating between the two heavens, John and Isaiah were also specific in mentioning a new earth. I find that interesting. Maybe you do too. If the main point of their writings was to communicate that we will someday get to spend eternity with God in His dwelling place, why wouldn't they just focus on heaven? Why specifically mention that the "first earth had passed away" and given way to a "new earth" (Rev. 21:1; Isa. 65:17; 66:22)?

I believe the answer is as simple as it sounds: because the new heaven and the new earth that both men mention are not two different places but one. This means heaven and earth come together as one! Just as God longs for the day the bride (us) and Bridegroom (Jesus) can be together as one, He cannot wait for the day when there is no separation between heaven and earth. God is a god of unity, and He longs for His creation to fully reflect His image and His glory. So in the day when the new heaven and new earth merge together, Jesus' prayer will be completely fulfilled as He prayed, "Your kingdom come; Your will be done on earth, as it is in heaven" (Matt. 6:10). All of God's creation will truly be unified as one.

Paul referred to this in Ephesians when he described the mystery of God's will "as a plan for the fullness of time, to unite all things in Christ, which are in heaven and on earth" (Eph. 1:10). How incredible! The Father's ultimate plan was that everything in the universe—heaven and earth—would become one in and through His Son, Yeshua.

Consider this: As I stated earlier, many people perceive heaven as a purely spiritual state and that when we get there we will simply be spiritual beings floating around in some type of spiritual space. But the truth is, we will have physical bodies in this new heaven and new earth. They will certainly be different from the bodies we currently have, but they will be bodies nonetheless—and perfect ones at that!

First Corinthians 15:53 says the perishable part of us—which would include our bodies—will become imperishable, and our mortal parts will become immortal. This verse alone could stand as proof that we will have physical bodies in the new heaven, albeit not of flesh but nevertheless bodies. We will have bodies in the future heaven because God made us to live in dimensions. When God originally created mankind, He created us in His own image—spirit, soul, and body. Likewise, in the new heaven we will fully reflect Him—spirit, soul, and body.

The testimonies we have from Ezekiel and John reveal to us that the Jesus they saw in heaven was complete with a body. In Ezekiel 1 the prophet saw a vision of Jesus in heaven "as the appearance of a man" (v. 26), and he described the Lord from the waist up as having a glory "as glowing metal" and from the waist down as "the appearance of fire" (v. 27).

All around this Man, who sat on something like a throne, was "the appearance of the rainbow that is in the cloud on a day of rain" (v. 28). John likewise saw the Lord in heaven *sitting* upon His throne, *standing* before the throne, *holding* a scroll in His right hand, and doing other physical actions that require a body (Rev. 4:2; 5:6–8).

The Bible clearly indicates that heaven will have a supernatural, physical element. John said, "I turned to *see* the voice that spoke" (Rev. 1:12, emphasis added). We will have real bodies. And heaven is a real place with real, measurable dimensions. Why else would one of the angels in Revelation 21 take John up "to a great and high mountain" to show him the New Jerusalem (v. 10), and why would John then describe this heavenly city with such specific physical dimensions? Indeed Revelation 21 details not only the city's exact length, width, and height (v. 16) but also a two-hundred-foot surrounding wall built of jasper, adorned with precious jewels (vv. 17–20), and containing twelve gates (vv. 12–14).

John describes heaven once again as a tangible place with a physical dimensionality to it, although it will not be of this world. Even as heaven is a supernatural, physical place, likewise as Paul said, we will have supernatural but real bodies.

## THE FINAL EMMANUEL

It's likely that I have presented some new ideas for you in this chapter. Some of these concepts about heaven may be challenging, while others may seem so radical they are hard for you to believe. Regardless of how these ideas are received, I pray that I have presented God's Word accurately.

But let me also offer a reminder. Paul said, "For now we see as through a glass, dimly, but then, face to face" (1 Cor. 13:12).

Stated another way, our current vision and understanding can be a little blurry sometimes, especially when discussing eternal matters. Few things speak of eternity as much as heaven, which means none of us has full understanding of exactly what heaven will be like. I am not foolish enough to think that I know everything there is to know about heaven, or that my perspective is flawless.

What I do know is that God's Word is our ultimate truth. Believers may differ on the specifics of heaven, but at the end of the day I believe the main point—the truth we can all agree on regarding heaven—is expressed in Revelation 21:3–4 (emphasis added):

> And I heard a loud voice from heaven, saying, "Look! The tabernacle of God is with men, and *He will dwell with them*. They shall be His people, and *God Himself will be with them and be their God*. 'God shall wipe away all tears from their eyes. There shall be no more death.' Neither shall there be any more sorrow nor crying nor pain, for the former things have passed away."

What is the ultimate point? That God will dwell with us! Remember, God's longing since creation was to be with His creation, His people. That's us! He desires a people who desire Him. In Moses' time the Israelites rejected His offer to come close and be with them; they preferred to keep a safe distance from this awesome, holy God (Exod. 20:19). So God stayed near to them through a tabernacle system. He later tried to come close through His prophets, but they too were shunned or ignored by Israel.

Although God's plan to be one with His people was

partially fulfilled at Yeshua's first coming, the Israelites rejected Him, just as they had in the past. Yet God's longing to be one with His people will be fulfilled in the last days when all Israel cries out to Yeshua and recognizes Him as the Messiah when He returns. Again, this will usher in the millennial age, and everything will climax with a new heaven and a new earth. God will make His tabernacle with us (Rev. 21:3)—and this time it will be *forever*!

Do you see it? The Lord wants to be with us just as a bride-groom wants to be with his bride. As the bride-to-be we, the church, are currently betrothed to Him, and He has gone to prepare a place for us—a home in heaven. Jesus said, "In My Father's house are many dwelling places. If it were not so, I would have told you. I am going to prepare a place for you. And if I go and prepare a place for you, I will come again and receive you to Myself, that where I am, you may be also" (John 14:2–3).

When the Lord returns He will marry us, take us away into this home, and then give us the fullness of Himself at the marriage supper of the Lamb. We will then live with Him in His house forever and ever. Amen!

## TURNED TOWARD HEAVEN

I like to think about heaven. I like imagining what it will be like. I love trying to wrap my mind around the concept of spending eternity with God. But at the end of all my thoughts and imaginations I always arrive at the same place: Being in heaven is all about knowing, being known by, and being loved by Him.

When I truly consider the reality of heaven, it puts every-thing else in perspective. I believe you will find the same thing true in your life. When we realize that heaven is an actual place awaiting us, then the temporal things surrounding us—our current problems and trials, or what we anxiously cling to and hold so dear—seem to lose their grip on us. I am not talking about losing ourselves in a make-believe world or a choose-your-own-fantasy version of the afterlife; I am talking about dwelling on the fact that heaven is real and that as God's children we will be there sooner than we think.

As a young believer I often heard the hymn "Turn Your Eyes Upon Jesus," which at that time was a staple for revival meetings, altar calls, worship services, and prayer meetings alike. Almost a century after it was first written, the chorus still has profound meaning, largely because of its simple yet powerful truth: "Turn your eyes upon Jesus / Look full in His wonderful face / And the things of earth will grow strangely dim / In the light of His glory and grace."[4]

Several years ago these words rang truer than ever in my life. I was in Haiti on a ministry trip when I received an unexpected phone call from my doctor back home, who knew I was abroad at the time. "I don't want to alarm you," she began, "but when you return from your trip, I'd like for you to come back into my office. The results from your blood test show you have low iron in your blood, and there are some things we need to check on." I could hear the concern in her voice, and since I had just been in her office days before leaving for Haiti, the fact that she called during my trip added to the gravity. When I went online and researched symptoms for low iron in your blood, I discovered why: One of the possible causes was cancer.

"I could die," I thought. "This might actually be the end of my life."

Most people would expect such news to be like a punch in the stomach. But in that moment I experienced one of the most beautiful feelings I have ever had. It was like an ocean of God's love washed over my soul, and I felt an indescribable mixture of peace, relief, and joy in what seemed like a never-ending exhale. I would be released from all the struggles of this world and all the burdens I carried. I had labored on this earth long and hard, yet now I would finally see Jesus face-to-face. I would meet the One I adored and served all these years—at last!

Obviously I didn't die. But that moment—when the things of this earth grew strangely dim in the light of the possibility of seeing Jesus—has never left me, and I hold on to the reality that I will see Him in heaven soon.

Paul said it this way: "For I consider that the sufferings of this present time are not worthy to be compared with the glory which shall be revealed to us" (Rom. 8:18). And in 2 Corinthians 4:17 he said, "Our light affliction, which lasts but for a moment, works for us a far more exceeding and eternal weight of glory." Whatever trials, troubles, and suffering we have are not only momentary, but Paul even called them "light" compared with the weight and glory of what awaits us in heaven. If we can keep this in perspective when we encounter difficult times, and if we can keep our eyes fixed on Jesus, we will be able to endure anything through God's grace. And we will not be disappointed!

# THE FINAL WORD

Notice that I said *when* we encounter difficult times, not *if* we encounter difficult times. We will face tough times—that is a certainty in this life. Jesus promised trials to anyone who follows Him: "In this world you will have trouble" (John 16:33, NIV). And He inspired David to say, "Many are the afflictions of the righteous, but the LORD delivers him out of them all" (Ps. 34:19).

Much of what we have covered in this book deals with trouble and, more specifically, how the end times will be filled with great trouble. As we have studied the Book of Revelation, we have seen that there will be a season of tribulation that the Hebrew Bible calls Jacob's trouble—calamity for Israel—that will jump-start the last days. During this time the earth will experience more calamity than ever before. I believe this season is beginning now, for Israel and the entire world, and storm clouds continue to darken the horizon.

As we delved further into topics in Revelation, such as the Antichrist's emergence, God's judgments and wrath, and Armageddon, we discovered that what will begin as turmoil will become far, far worse. The dark clouds eventually will blanket the world with such complete darkness that even the cosmos will lose their light. Yet all this must take place for Yeshua to return.

But our study of Revelation also revealed that the grace of Jesus will be sufficient for His own during this time. For while evil rises and nations become more godless, a remnant will grow stronger and eventually be rescued when the Messiah returns (Dan. 7:25; 11:35). Yeshua's second coming at Armageddon will begin a sequence of events including the church's rapture, Israel's salvation, and the most glorious event in history, the "marriage supper of the Lamb." Believers can hold on to the hope that our union with the Lord will fulfill every longing we have ever had on the earth—and then some! This state of complete ecstasy will continue from the present heaven into a new heaven to come, where we will spend eternity with our God.

I do not expect you to understand everything we have covered. I don't even fully understand it! I have studied Revelation for years, and I am still learning new things each time I read John's account. As I stated in the introduction to this book, the most important thing when trying to understand the content of Revelation is to stick with it, to not give up when things don't make sense or are difficult to understand. This is a vital book of the Bible for us today. I hope you have seen how John's vision affirms the hundreds of end-times prophecies delivered through the Hebrew prophets of the Tanakh. God's Word is truly amazing in its harmony, down to the smallest details.

It is easy to get bogged down in those details and forget the main message of Revelation. We have a Savior who is coming back. He will return as the glorious, victorious King of kings and will immediately prove His power and authority by ridding the earth of all evil and wickedness. As we long for that day, we can actually hasten its arrival with our prayers—calling our Savior to come—and with our preparedness. Much of the church today does not understand this because they never bother to read Revelation or they lack the revelation to understand Revelation. We must understand this crucial book, however; it is the church's guidebook for the end times. God gave it to us so that we would be prepared for the unique, troubling season to come.

Imagine you are a football player who has come to the sidelines for some rest between quarters of an intense game. The score is tied, and the fourth quarter is about to begin. Your coach walks up to you, hands you a playbook, and says, "Study this—you're going to need it to win the game." As he walks away, you scan through the playbook's pages and discover that not only does it list the final outcome of the game, but it also has the details of every play that will be made to reach that score. It even tells you what you need to do on each of those plays. What?

Do you think you would pay attention to a book like that? Of course you would! Sadly, much of the church today is not paying attention to the Book of Revelation. They are convinced things will work themselves out, and since Jesus will win in the end, they assume they can just go through life doing their best as a good follower of Christ. You obviously do not fall in that category since you have read this book. But like a coach spurring his players on before the fourth quarter starts, I want to encourage you. Things are about to get tough. At times it will seem like our side is losing. But stay strong, and stay the course. Don't give up, both in your pursuit to understand this book and in the faith. Jesus is coming soon—He really is. When things in this world continue to go from bad to worse, remind yourself of what Revelation says. The tribulation is part of God's plan, yet amid trouble God will give us the grace to overcome and to shine like beacons of hope in a growing storm.

Yeshua our Savior is coming back for us, His bride. He awaits a bride who is ready for His return, and until she is,

He will not return. That means our top priority must be to prepare. You and I must do whatever it takes to be ready for Jesus' return, and the good news is that the Holy Spirit can and will guide us. If you need to reprioritize your lifestyle to make Him the centerpiece, then do it today. If you need to deal with sin issues in your life that keep you entangled, then He is waiting to help with that. If you need to recommit your life to Jesus, turning away from your past and starting on a new path with Him, act with urgency. Whatever you need to do, do it now while there is still time to prepare!

May the Lord strengthen us to turn our eyes completely to Him and await His return. He has promised that He is coming soon. And He is faithful to His promises.

Come, Lord Jesus—come!

If you enjoyed this book and believe other people would be helped by reading it, please leave a review on Amazon.

# NOTES

## Introduction

1. "Deadliest terrorist attacks worldwide from 1970 to January 2024, by number of fatalities and perpetrator," Statista, accessed April 17, 2024, https://www.statista.com/statistics/1330395/deadliest-terrorist-attacks-worldwide-fatalities/.
2. Emily Feng, "China's Millennial and Gen Z Workers Are Having to Lower Their Economic Expectations," NPR, January 16, 2024, https://www.npr.org/2024/01/16/1217223941/china-youth-unemployment-slow-economic-growth.
3. "Global Economy Set for Weakest Half-Decade Performance in 30 Years," World Bank, January 9, 2024, https://www.worldbank.org/en/news/press-release/2024/01/09/global-economic-prospects-january-2024-press-release.
4. Clay Dillow, "Iran Nuclear Deal Could Prompt Regional Arms Race," *Fortune*, July 17, 2015, http://fortune.com/2015/07/17/iran-nuclear-deal-arms.
5. Elizabeth Chuck, "Fact Sheet: Who Has Nuclear Weapons, and How Many Do They Have?," NBC News, March 31, 2016, http://www.nbcnews.com/news /world/fact-sheet-who-has-nuclear-weapons-how-many-do-they-n548481.
6. "North Korea," NTI, accessed April 18, 2024, https://www.nti.org/countries/north-korea/; "Iran," accessed April 18, 2024, https://www.nti.org/countries/iran.
7. "PTSD, Depression, and Anxiety Nearly Doubles in Israel in Aftermath of Hamas Attack," Columbia University Department of Psychiatry, January 5, 2024, https://www.columbiapsychiatry.org/news/ptsd-depression-and-anxiety-nearly-doubles-israel-aftermath-october-7-2023-terrorist-attack.
8. "Americans Express Worry Over Personal Safety in Annual Anxiety and Mental Health Poll," American Psychiatric Association, May 10, 2023, https://www.psychiatry.org/news-room/news-releases/annual-anxiety-and-mental-health-poll-2023.
9. "An Economic Meltdown Is the Doomsday Americans Fear the Most. Here's Why," Ipsos, April 8, 2024, https://www.ipsos.com/en-us/economic-meltdown-doomsday-americans-fear-most-heres-why.
10. "Global Citizens Achieve Near Consensus: The World Is Becoming More Dangerous," Ipsos, November 18, 2023, https://www.ipsos.com/en-us/halifax-report-2023-conflict.

11. "Global Citizens Achieve Near Consensus: The World Is Becoming More Dangerous," Ipsos.

12. Jonathan Landry Cruse, "Why the Bible Talks About the End Times So Much," March 29, 2023, https://tabletalkmagazine. com/posts/why-the-bible-talks-about-the-end-times-so-much.

13. George V. Wigram, *The Englishman's Greek Concordance of the New Testament: Coded With Strong's Concordance Numbers* (Peabody, MA: Hendrickson Publishers, 1996), viewed at http:// biblehub.com/greek/prosdoko_ntas_4328.htm.

14. Jewish Population Rises to 15.7 Million Worldwide in 2023," Jewish Agency for Israel, September 15, 2023, https://www. jewishagency.org/jewish-population-rises-to-15-7-million-worldwide-in-2023/

## CHAPTER 1

1. Eric Lyons and Kyle Butt, "Legends of the Flood," Apologetics Press, November 1. 2003, https://apologeticspress.org/ apcontent.aspx?category=9&article=64; see also John D. Morris, "Why Does Nearly Every Culture Have a Tradition of a Global Flood?," Institute Creation Research, September 1, 2001,https://www.icr.org/article/why-does-nearly-every-culture-have-tradition-globa; and Monty White, "Flood Legends: The Significance of a World of Stories Based on Truth," Answers, March 29, 2007, https://answersingenesis.org/the-flood/flood-legends/flood-legends/.

2. Jenna Millman, Bryan Taylor, and Lauren Effron, "Evidence Noah's Biblical Flood Happened, Says Robert Ballard," GMA, December 5, 2012, https://www.goodmorningamerica.com/ news/story/evidence-suggests-biblical-great-flood-noahs-time-happened-17884533.

## CHAPTER 2

1. Rick Noack, "A 94-Year-Old Former Nazi Guard Stands Accused of Helping to Murder 170,000 People," *Washington Post*, February 11, 2016, , https://www.washingtonpost.com/ news/worldviews/wp/2016/02/11/a-94-year-old-former-nazi-guard-stands-accused-of-helping-to-murder-170000-people/.

2. Ian Kershaw, *Hitler: A Biography* (New York: W. W. Norton & Company, 2008), 93.

3. *The Columbia Encyclopedia*, Sixth Edition, s.v. "Hitler, Adolf," June 2, 2024, www.encyclopedia.com/people/history/german-history-biographies/adolf-hitlerhttp://www.encyclopedia.com/ topic /Adolf_Hitler.aspx#4.

4. C. N. Trueman, "Jews in Nazi Germany," The History Learning Site, March 9, 2015, http:// www.historylearningsite.

co.uk/nazi-germany/jews-in-nazi-germany/; see also Adolf Hitler, *Mein Kampf* (Boston: Mariner Books, 1999).

5. Blake Stilwell, "Memorial Day by the Numbers: Casualties of Every American War," Military.com, May 15, 2020, https://www.military.com/memorial-day/how-many-us-militay-members-died-each-american-war.html; Jeff Diamant, Besheer Mohamed, and Rebecca Leppert, "What the Data Says About Abortion in the U.S.," Pew Research Center, March 25, 2024, https://www.pewresearch.org/short-reads/2024/03/25/what-the-data-says-about-abortion-in-the-us/#how-many-abortions-are-there-in-the-us-each-year; Juliana Kim, "No Region Is 'Immune' as the Number of People in 'Modern Slavery' Climbs to 50 Million," NPR, September 13, 2022, https://www.npr.org/sections/goatsandsoda/2022/09/13/1122714064/modern-slavery-global-estimate-increase; Henry Louis Gates Jr., "How Many Slaves Landed in the U.S.?," PBS, accessed May 3, 2024, https://www.pbs.org/wnet/african-americans-many-rivers-to-cross/history/how-many-slaves-landed-in-the-us.

6. This is based on Exodus 12:37 and Numbers 1:45–46, 11:21, and 26:51 and uses the widely accepted estimation that the total population was at least two to three times the number of adult men recorded (which these scriptures indicate). An interesting argument for this can be found at: http://www.bible.ca/archeology/bible-archeology-exodus-route-population-of-jews-hebrews.htm.

7. Bible Hub, s.v. "maranatha," accessed June 11, 2024, http://biblehub.com/greek/3134.htm.

## CHAPTER 3

1. "World War I: Aftermath," Holocaust Encyclopedia, United States Holocaust Memorial Museum, accessed June 2, 2024, https://encyclopedia.ushmm.org/content/en/article/world-war-i-aftermath.

2. "The Boycott of Jewish Businesses," Holocaust Encyclopedia, United States Holocaust Memorial Museum, accessed June 2, 2024, https://encyclopedia.ushmm.org/content/en/article/boycott-of-jewish-businesses.

3. "Röhm Purge," Holocaust Encyclopedia, United States Holocaust Memorial Museum, accessed June 2, 2024, https://encyclopedia.ushmm.org/content/en/article/roehm-purge.

4. Milton Kestenberg, "Legal Aspects of Child Persecution During the Holocaust," *Journal of the American Academy of Child Psychiatry* 24 (1985): 381–84.

5. National Right to Life, "Reported Annual Abortions 1973-2019," accessed May 3, 2024, https://www.nrlc.org/uploads/factsheets/FS01AbortionintheUS.pdf; Kyle Morris and Sam Dorman, "Over 63 Million Abortions Have Occurred in the US Since Roe v. Wade Decision in 1973," Fox News, May 4, 2022, https://www.foxnews.com/politics/abortions-since-roe-v-wade.

6. "Putin Warns Again That Russia Is Ready to Use Nuclear Weapons If Its Sovereignty Is Threatened," The Associated Press, March 13, 2024, https://apnews.com/article/russia-ukraine-war-putin-nuclear-weapons-82ced2419d93ae-733161b56fbd9b477d.

7. Samantha Kamman, "Removing Trans-Identified Child From Catholic Parents' Home Sets 'Dangerous Precedent': Attorney," *The Christian Post*, February 20, 2024, https://www.christianpost.com/news/parents-who-lost-custody-of-child-ask-supreme-court-to-hear-case.html.

8. Peter J. Smith, "Germany Jails Eight Christian Fathers for Removing Children From Sex-Ed Class," LifeSiteNews, December 11, 2009, https://www.lifesitenews.com/news/germany-jails-eight-christian-fathers-for-removing-children-from-sex-ed-cla; "Swedish Anti-Abortion Midwife Sues County," *The Local*, July 11, 2014, http://www.thelocal.se/20140711/anti-abortion-nurse-takes-firing-case-to-court; "Sweden Abortion: Nurses Fail in European Court Case," BBC, March 10, 2020, https://www.bbc.com/news/world-europe-51874119; Natalia Dueholm, "Lynched, Fined, and Dismissed: An Interview With Poland's Dr. Bogdan Chazan," LifeSiteNews, July 18, 2014, https://www.lifesitenews.com/news/lynched-fined-and-dismissed-an-interview-with-polands-dr.-bogdan -chazan.

9. Tracy Munsil, "AWVI 2020 Survey: 1 in 3 US Adults Embrace Salvation Through Jesus; More Believe It Can Be 'Earned,'" Arizona Christian University, August 4, 2020, https://www.arizonachristian.edu/2020/08/04/1-in-3-us-adults-embrace-salvation-through-jesus-more-believe-it-can-be-earned/.

10. "Anugrah Kumar, "60% of Adults Under 40 Say Jesus Isn't Only Way To Salvation; Equal to Buddha, Muhammad," Christian Post, August 22, 2021, https://www.christianpost.com/news/60-of-young-adults-say-jesus-isnt-the-only-way-to-salvation.html.

11. Frank Swain, "Why I Want a Microchip Implant," BBC Future, February 10, 2014, https://www.bbc.com/future/article/20140209-why-i-want-a-microchip-implant; Katharine Latham, "The Microchip Implants That Let You Pay With

Your Hand," BBC, April 10, 2022, https://www.bbc.com/news/business-61008730.

12. Latham, "The Microchip Implants That Let You Pay With Your Hand."

13. Martin Korte, PhD, "The Impact of the Digital Revolution on the Human Brain and Behavior: Where Do We Stand?" *Dialogues Clinical Neuroscience* 22, no. 2 (June 2020): 101–111, doi: 10.31887/DCNS.2020.22.2/mkorte.

14. Kevin Roose, "AI Poses 'Risk of Extinction,' Industry Leaders Warn," May 30, 2023, https://www.nytimes.com/2023/05/30/technology/ai-threat-warning.html; Rishi Iyengar, "The U.N. Gets the World to Agree on AI Safety," March 21, 2024, https://foreignpolicy.com/2024/03/21/un-ai-regulation-vote-resolution-artifical-intelligence-human-rights.

15. Clare Duffy and Ramishah Maruf, "Elon Musk Warns AI Could Cause 'Civilization Destruction' Even as He Invests in It," CNN, April 17, 2023, https://www.cnn.com/2023/04/17/tech/elon-musk-ai-warning-tucker-carlson/index.html.

16. Walter Isaacson, *Steve Jobs* (New York: Simon & Schuster, 2011), 69; see also Michelle Starr, "10 Facts About the Apple-1, the Machine That Made Computing History," CNET, May 29, 2024, http://www.cnet.com/news/apple-1-the%20-machine-that-made-computing-history/, http://www.cnet.com/news/apple-1-the-machine-that-made-computing-history/.

### CHAPTER 4

1. Vincent J. Schodolski, "Soviet Bread Prices Skyrocket by 600 Percent," *Chicago Tribune*, November 13, 1991, https://www.chicagotribune.com/1991/11/13/soviet-bread-prices-skyrocket-by-600/.

2. Linette Lopez, "How Russia's Billionaire Oligarchs Got So Very Rich," *Business Insider*, March 24, 2013, https://www.businessinsider.in/how-russias-billionaire-oligarchs-got-so-very-rich/articleshow/21229736.cms.

3. Justin D. Long, "More Martyrs Now Than Then?" John Mark Ministries, January 5, 2003, http://www.jmm.org.au/articles/2904.htm.

4. "Almost Half of Evangelical Leaders Have Been Cancelled," NAE, September 8, 2022, https://www.nae.org/evangelical-leaders-cancelled/.

5. Rahem D. Hamid and Elias J. Schisgall, "More Than Three-Quarters of Surveyed Harvard Faculty Identify as Liberal," *Harvard Crimson*, May 22, 2023, https://www.thecrimson.com/article/2023/5/22/faculty-survey-2023-politics.

6. "Evidence," NASA, accessed April 29, 2024, https://science.nasa.gov/climate-change/evidence/.

7. Andrea Thompson, "A Running List of Record-Breaking Natural Disasters in 2020," *Scientific American*, December 22, 2020, https://www.scientificamerican.com/article/a-running-list-of-record-breaking-natural-disasters-in-2020/; "2023 Was the Warmest Year in the Modern Temperature Record," NOAA National Centers for Environmental Information, January 17, 2024, https://www.climate.gov/news-features/featured-images/2023-was-warmest-year-modern-temperature-record#:~:text=Details,decade%20(2014%E2%80%932023.

8. Dylan Thuras, "Hail No: An Account of the World's Biggest, Deadliest Hailstorms," *Atlas Obscura*, September 26, 2010, http://www.atlasobscura.com/articles/hail-no-an-account-of-the-worlds-biggest-deadliest-hailstorms; "1888: Orange-Sized Hail Reported in India," History.com, accessed June 11, 2024, https://web.archive.org/web/20121105012256/http://www.history.com/this-day-in-history/orange-sized-hail-reported-in-india.

9. Christopher C. Burt, "The Worst Wild Fires in World History," Weather Underground, June 17, 2011, https://www.wunderground.com/blog/weatherhistorian/the-worst-wild-fires-in-world-history.html; see also "12 of the Worst Wildfires in U.S. History," MSN.com, accessed June 11, 2024, https://www.msn.com/en-us/weather/photos/12-of-the-worst-wildfires-in-us-history/ss-AAhOYy3#image=12.

10. Andrea Thompson, "A Running List of Record-Breaking Natural Disasters in 2020."

11. David Helvarg, "Opinion: Florida's Sea Temperature Hit 101. What Does That Mean for the World's Oceans?" *Los Angeles Times*, August 1, 2023, https://www.latimes.com/opinion/story/2023-08-01/florida-heat-wave-ocean-coral-bleached-climate-crisis.

12. "Herpes Simplex Virus," World Health Organization, April 5, 2023, https://www.who.int/news-room/fact-sheets/detail/herpes-simplex-virus#:~:text=Key%20facts,main%20cause%20of%20genital%20herpes.

CHAPTER 6

1. David Noel Freedman, ed., *Eerdmans Dictionary of the Bible* (Grand Rapids, MI: Eerdmans Publishing Co., 2000), 681.

CHAPTER 8

1. *Merriam-Webster*, s.v. "grieve," accessed June 11, 2024, https://www.merriam-webster.com/dictionary/grieve.

2. Bible Hub, s.v. *"guwl,"* accessed June 11, 2024, http://biblehub.
com/hebrew/1523.htm; Blue Letter Bible, accessed June 11,
2024, https://www.blueletterbible.org/lang/Lexicon/Lexicon.
cfm?strongs=H1523&t=KJV.

3. Matthew George Easton, "Entry for Baali," *Illustrated Bible Dictionary,* third edition (Nashville, TN: Thomas Nelson, 1897).

CHAPTER 9

1. "Jewish Population Rises to 15.7 Million Worldwide in 2023,"
The Jewish Agency for Israel.

2. Alan Cooperman, "10 Key Findings About Jewish Americans," Pew Research Center, May 11, 2021, https://www.
pewresearch.org/short-reads/2021/05/11/10-key-findings-
about-jewish-americans/; "A Portrait of Jewish Americans,"
Pew Research Center, October 1, 2013, http://www.pew forum.
org/2013/10/01/jewish-american-beliefs-attitudes-culture-
survey/; "Israel's Religiously Divided Society," Pew Research
Center, March 8, 2016, http://www.pewforum .org/2016/03/08/
israels-religiously-divided-society/.

3. Gershon Nerel, "How Many Messianic Jews Actually Live
in Israel?," *Israel Today,* February 18, 2022, https://www.
israeltoday.co.il/read/how-many-messianic-jews-actually-
live-in-israel/; "Findings of New Research on the Messianic
Movement in Israel," One for Israel, accessed April 18, 2024,
https://www.oneforisrael.org/bible-based-teaching-from-
israel/findings-of-new-research-on-the-messianic-movement-
in-israel.

4. "Ten Lost Tribes of Israel," *Encyclopædia Britannica,* accessed
June 11, 2024, https://www.britannica.com/topic/Ten-Lost-
Tribes-of-Israel.

5. "Statistical Abstract of Israel 2023," Central Bureau of Statistics, August 30, 2023, https://www.cbs.gov.il/he/publications/
doclib/2023/2.shnatonpopulation/st02_02.pdf; "Comparisons
Between Jews in Israel and the U.S.," Pew Research Center,
March 8, 2016, https://www.pewresearch.org/religion/2016/03/08/
comparisons-between-jews-in-israel-and-the-u-s/.

6. Ibrahim Omer, "Evidence Mounts of Ancient Jewish Roots
of Beta Israel Ethiopian Jewry," Genetic Literacy Project,
June 16, 2015, https://geneticliteracyproject.org/2015/06/16/
evidence-mounts-of-ancient-jewish-roots-of-beta-israel-ethi-
opian-jewry/; see also Sharon Begley, "Genetic Study Offers
Clues to History of North Africa's Jews," Reuters, August 7,
2012, https://www.reuters.com/article/idUSL2E8J63VN/.

7. Y. Y. Waldman, Arjun Biddanda et al., "The Genetics of Bene
Israel From India Reveals Both Substantial Jewish and Indian

Ancestry," *PLoS ONE 11* (3): e0152056, abstract viewed June 11, 2024, at http://journals.plos.org/plosone/article?id=10.1371/journal.pone.0152056.

CHAPTER 10

1. Emma Robinson, "Driver Who Ignored 14 Speeding Tickets Is Ordered to Pay Out More Than £10,000," *Basildon Canvey Southend Echo*, June 22, 2016, http://www.echo-news.co.uk/news/14573131.Driver_who_ignored_14_speeding_tickets_is_ordered_to_pay_out_more_than ____10_000/?ref=mr&lp=9; Simon Murfitt, "Essex Driver Fined £10,500 for Ignoring 14 Speeding Tickets," *Brentwood Gazette*.
2. Brother Lawrence, *The Practice of the Presence of God* (Alachua, FL: Bridge-Logos, 1999).
3. Brother Lawrence, *The Practice of the Presence of God* (New Kensington, PA: Whitaker House, 1982), 37.
4. Rick Joyner, *The Final Quest* (Charlotte, NC: MorningStar Publications, 1996).
5. Walter Mischel, Ebbe B. Ebbesen, Antonette Raskoff Zeiss, "Cognitive and Attentional Mechanisms in Delay of Gratification," *Journal of Personality and Social Psychology* 21, no. 2 (1972): 204–218.
6. James Clear, "40 Years of Stanford Research Found That People With This One Quality Are More Likely to Succeed," updated July 2, 2016, https://www.huffpost.com/entry/40-years-of-stanford-rese_b_7707444.

CHAPTER 11

1. "Views on the Afterlife," Pew Research Center, November 23, 2021, https://www.pewresearch.org/religion/2021/11/23/views-on-the-afterlife/.
2. Albert L. Winseman, "Eternal Destinations: Americans Believe in Heaven, Hell," Gallup, May 25, 2004, http://www.gallup.com/poll/11770/eternal-destinations-americans-believe-heaven-hell.aspx.
3. "About Bill and Annette Wiese," Soul Choice Ministries, accessed June 3, 2024, https://soulchoiceministries.org/about-bill-and-annette-wiese/.
4. Bill Wiese, *23 Minutes in Hell* (Lake Mary, FL: Charisma House, 2006), 60.
5. Wiese, *23 Minutes in Hell*, 99–100, 165–192.
6. Wiese, *23 Minutes in Hell*, 99–100, 165–192.
7. "Deepest Part of the Ocean," Geology.com, accessed June 3, 2024, https://geology.com/records/deepest-part-of-the-ocean.shtml.

8. Jason Palmer, "Earth's Core Far Hotter Than Thought," BBC News, April 26, 2013, https://www.bbc.com/news/science-environment-22297915.

9. Janko Azkoyen, "Kola Superdeep Borehole," Atlas Obscura, November 10, 2009, https://www.atlasobscura.com/places/kola-superdeep-borehole.

10. Barbara Maranzani, "The Hottest Day on Earth, 100 Years Ago," History.com, July 10, 2013, , https://www.history.com/news/the-hottest-day-on-earth-100-years-ago; Tom Leonard, "The 9/11 Victims America Wants to Forget: The 200 Jumpers Who Flung Themselves From the Twin Towers Who Have Been 'Airbrushed From History,'" DailyMail.com, September 11, 2011, https://www.dailymail.co.uk/news/article-2035720/9-11-jumpers-America-wants-forget-victims-fell-Twin-Towers; "FAQs—NIST WTC Towers Investigation," NIST Engineering Laboratory, accessed June 3, 2024, https://www.nist.gov/el/faqs-nist-wtc-towers-investigation; "Special Report: Debunking the 9/11 Conspiracy Theories of the World Trade Center," Popular Mechanics, September 11, 2023, http://www.popularmechanics.com/military/a6384 /debunking-911-myths-world-trade-center/.

11. Wiese, 23 Minutes in Hell, xxi–xxii.

12. Wiese, 23 Minutes in Hell, 8–9.

13. Richard Eby, Caught Up Into Paradise (Grand Rapids, MI: Fleming H. Revell Co., 1990), 229–230.

14. Michelle Wilson, "A Wake-up Call From Hell," CBN, December 10, 2022, https://www2.cbn.com/article/not-selected/wake-call-hell.

15. Josephine Vivaldo, "Former Non-Christian: My Time in Hell," The Christian Post, May 3, 2011, https://www.christianpost.com/news/former-atheist-my-time-in-hell.html.

16. Sylvia Johnson and Rob Wallace, "Touching Heaven and Hell," ABC News, July 9, 2007, http://abcnews.go.com/2020/story?id=3359251&page=1.

17. Curtis Kelley, Bound to Lose Destined to Win (CreateSpace, 2011), 62–63.

18. Saint Teresa of Avila, The Life of St. Teresa of Avila (New York, NY: Cosimo, 2006), 252–253.

19. Wiese, 23 Minutes in Hell, 45.

CHAPTER 12

1. "Aliyah to Israel," Israel Science and Technology, accessed November 23, 2016, http://www.science.co.il/Aliyah.php; Blue Letter Bible, s.v. "ʿălîyâ," accessed June 10, 2024, https://www.blueletterbible.org/lexicon/h5944/kjv/wlc/0-1/.

## CHAPTER 13

1. Helder Sanches, "Contact—'They Should Have Sent a Poet,'" YouTube, July 18, 2011, https://www.youtube.com/watch?v=3deNVM3EWIc.
2. Sanches, "Contact—'They Should Have Sent a Poet.'"
3. M. G. Easton, "Heaven," *Illustrated Bible Dictionary*, third edition (Nashville, TN: Thomas Nelson, 1897).
4. Helen H. Lemmel, "Turn Your Eyes Upon Jesus," Hynmal.net, accessed June 11, 2024, https://www.hymnal.net/en/hymn/h/645Public domain.

# DISCOVERING THE JEWISH JESUS

## CONNECT WITH RABBI SCHNEIDER

www.DiscoveringTheJewishJesus.com

/Discovering the Jewish Jesus with Rabbi Schneider

facebook.com/rabbischneider

@RabbiSchneider

Roku—Discovering the Jewish Jesus

Apple TV—Discovering the Jewish Jesus

Amazon App—Discovering the Jewish Jesus

Podcast—Discovering the Jewish Jesus

Search for Rabbi Schneider and Discovering the Jewish Jesus on your favorite platform.

For a complete list of Rabbi Schneider's television and radio broadcasts, visit www.DiscoveringTheJewishJesus.com.